SOCIO
Genera
Accession n
905341

✔ KT-231-852

LIBRARY
Tel: 01244 375444

The ... place Range, *Basingstoke*

CHESTER COLLEGE
ACC. No.	DEPT.
905341	
CLASS No.	
200.13 THO	
LIBRARY	

LONGMAN
London and New York

LONGMAN GROUP UK LIMITED
*Longman House, Burnt Mill, Harlow, Essex CM20 2JE, UK
and Associated Companies throughout the World.*

**Published in the United States of America
by Longman Inc., New York**

© **Longman Group Limited 1986**
*All rights reserved; no part of this publication
may be reproduced, stored in a retrieval system,
or transmitted in any form or by any means, electronic,
mechanical, photocopying, recording, or otherwise,
without the prior written permission of the Publishers.*
*First published 1986
Fourth impression 1989*
ISBN 0 582 35497 8

Set in 10/11 pt Bembo, Linotron 202

*Produced by Longman Singapore Publishers Pte Ltd
Printed in Singapore*

British Library Cataloguing in Publication Data

Thompson, Ian
   Religion. — (Sociology in focus)
   1. Religion and sociology
   I. Title   II. Series
   306'.6   BL60

ISBN 0-582-35497-8

Library of Congress Cataloguing in Publication Data

Thompson, Ian E.
   Religion.
   (Sociology in focus Series)
   Bibliography: p.
   Includes index.
   Summary: Identifies the themes, issues, and trends
of religion and discusses the relationship between sociology and
religion.
   1. Religion.   2. Religion and sociology
 [1. Religion.   2. Religion and sociology] I. Title.
II. Series
BL48.   T38   1985   306'.6   85-11929
ISBN 0-582-35497-8

Contents

Acknowledgements

We are indebted to Wadsworth Publishing Co for permission to reproduce extracts from *Religion: The Social Context* by M. B. McGuire.

Series introduction

Sociology in Focus aims to provide an up-to-date, coherent coverage of the main topics that arise on an introductory course in sociology. While the intention is to do justice to the intricacy and complexity of current issues in sociology, the style of writing has deliberately been kept simple. This is to ensure that the student coming to these ideas for the first time need not become lost in what can appear initially as jargon.

Each book in the series is designed to show something of the purpose of sociology and the craft of the sociologist. Throughout the different topic areas the interplay of theory, methodology and social policy have been highlighted, so that rather than sociology appearing as an unwieldy collection of facts, the student will be able to grasp something of the process whereby sociological understanding is developed. The format of the books is broadly the same throughout. Part one provides an overview of the topic as a whole. In part two the relevant research is set in the context of the theoretical, methodological and policy issues. The student is encouraged to make his or her own assessment of the various arguments, drawing on the statistical and reference material provided both here and at the end of the book. The final part of the book contains both statistical material and a number of 'Readings'. Questions have been provided in this section to direct students to analyse the materials presented in terms of both theoretical assumptions and methodological approaches. It is intended that this format should enable students to exercise their own sociological imaginations rather than to see sociology as a collection of universally accepted facts, which just have to be learned.

While each book in the series is complete within itself, the similarity of format ensures that the series as a whole provides an integrated and balanced introduction to sociology. It is intended that the text can be used both for individual and classroom study, while the inclusion of the variety of statistical and documentary materials lend themselves to both the preparation of essays and brief seminars.

PART 1

Introduction and overview

1 Religion: themes and issues

Imagine that you have just completed a short bus or train journey. How do you know whether the person next to you was not undergoing a deep religious experience? Were they praying? The person in front of you was clearly interested in the horoscope page of their newspaper. Does this have any significance when trying to assess whether they are religious? While such questions may seem an odd way to begin a book on the sociology of religion, they are central concerns. Not only do we need to define what is meant by 'religious', but we also require some measure of it.

This is far from easy. We need to take account of the wide variety of apparent 'religious' belief, but we also need some measure to assess its importance. While it may be relatively easy to measure car production in the United Kingdom, assessing religious beliefs presents us with rather more difficulties. Indeed, the different ways in which religion has been defined and measured has led to conflicting research findings.

Secularisation

While a variety of strategies have been used the basic problems of definition and measurement have remained. This is particularly well illustrated when looking at what has become known as the secularisation debate – the debate over whether religion has _Basic_ declined, both in terms of beliefs and practices, and in its _debate_ influence over our daily lives.

Those sociologist who have defined secularisation as a decline in organised religious participation point to statistical material to support their case (see Figures 7.1, 7.2 and 7.3 on pages 67–69). Statistics on church attendance, baptism, confirmation, marriages and the number of clergy, suggest that there is a marked decline. While there is an awareness that such statistics need to be treated with caution, it is generally accepted that religious participation in the major churches has declined.

However, even with such apparently strong evidence for secularisation, a number of criticisms have been made. Sociologists critical of such research have pointed to the need to look at the meanings behind such statistics. Can we assume that there is a connection between religious belief and church attendance? In previous years many people may have felt obliged to attend church despite the absence of any deeply held religious beliefs.

While there may have been a reduction in the number of people attending established church services, there has been a significant growth in other areas. For example, in the period 1975–1980 statistics suggest a three fold increase in the number of 'House Churches' (small groups of people worshipping together in houses rather than participating in church services), and a significant growth among groups such as Jehovah's Witnesses and the Church of Jesus Christ of Latter Day Saints (Mormons). Furthermore, other studies have pointed to the high percentage of people who claim to hold some form of religious belief. For example, a 1979 Gallup Poll showed that 76 per cent claimed to believe in God.

The situation is perhaps more complex when we consider the wide variety of ways in which secularisation has been defined and measured. While some have looked at church statistics, other indicators have been analysed, including the growth of 'scientific' thought and its effects on religious belief; the declining influence of the Church in such areas as social welfare, education and political processes; the Church's increased concern with secular activities and a decline in its religious dimension. What remains clear from all such research are the difficulties associated with defining and measuring religious factors, and although many would accept that there is some truth in the secularisation argument, Britain and other countries are far from being totally secular.

One example of the problem of definition can be seen in the case of 'broad' and 'narrow' definitions of religion. Those sociologists who define religion as a belief in a supernatural entity and link this to institutional religious organisations claim, perhaps with some justification, that religion is declining. Others however, who adopt a definition of constructing a set of 'universes of meaning' with which to interpret the world have arrived at different conclusions. Rather than seeing religion in decline they tend to point to a transformation of religion and a movement towards a more personal and private type. While it may be possible to conceive of indices to measure religion in the narrow sense, in the broader sense we have more difficulty. If religion has become more individualised and is defined as systems of meaning, not only is the analysis extremely complex, but also difficult to quantify.

Sects

Researchers have also pointed to the rapid growth of new religious movements in the last twenty-five years. The development of groups such as the Moonies and Krishna Consciousness have not only fuelled the secularisation debate, but have led to considerable research activity in their own right. While for some, like Bryan Wilson, such groups are dismissed as transient and volatile gestures in the face of secularising tendencies, for others such as Bellah they have the potential to change the nature of society – they offer the potential to achieve a society in which 'Priorities would shift away from endless accumulation of wealth and power to a greater concern for harmony with nature and between human beings.' (Bellah, 1976).

Such conflicting views not only illustrate different interpretations, but also reveal the problem of generalising about such movements. Various distinctions have been made including a seven-fold classification by Wilson and a distinction between world-affirming and world-rejecting sects by Wallis. While it is clear that if we are to understand and account for the wide variety of sects we need some typology, the present proliferation of labels and categories, coupled with arguments concerning whether a particular group is a sect or denomination, is in danger of clouding rather than clarifying the issues.

Considerable early research into sects suggested a close relationship between them and disadvantaged groups in society. In many ways this reflects the work of one of the founding fathers of sociology, **Max Weber** (1864–1920), who suggested that religious beliefs were closely related to social stratification. He suggested that the wealthy and fortunate would require a religion which justified, legitimated and explained their privileged position. The disadvantaged (and these may not only be the marginal groups in society, but also those who feel they are suffering 'relative deprivation'), seek a religion which promises them something better in this life or the world after. While the privileged and fortunate may join churches which are more likely to support the existing system and are integrated with it, the disadvantaged are more likely to belong to sects which tend to oppose society and cut themselves off from it. More recent research however, suggests that sects are not always the religions of the disadvantaged, although certain sects, such as Elim, may recruit from these groups. Furthermore, analysis of the new religious movements of the last twenty years or so, suggest a number of important differences between these and other sectarian developments in the past. In particular these new movements appear to be especially attractive to the young and also to those from relatively affluent backgrounds.

Religion and social integration

While Weber drew our attention to the variety of life experiences, the different meaning systems with which such groups operate, and therefore the different religious beliefs which may be held, **Emile Durkheim** (1858–1917), attempted to connect religious beliefs and practices with the characteristics of social groups on a societal level.

Durkheim believed that social life could only exist if values were shared and society integrated into a coherent whole. This 'value consensus' is achieved by shared values which are passed from generation to generation, frequently reinforced and legitimated. Religion is an important element of this process and not only provides a set of beliefs and practices which unite men together, but also provides 'categories of understanding' by which men can interpret and give meaning to the world.

Durkheim began his analysis of the function of religion by studying Australian Aborigines since their totemic religion represented the most 'elementary form of religious life'. Among Aborigine tribes there existed a number of sub-divisions or clans. Each clan was made up of members who felt they had a kinship bond, not based on ties of blood, but a shared name. The name, which was usually a species of animal or plant, was a totem or emblem which identified the clan.

The totem was a sacred object and various rituals and observances surrounded it. According to Durkheim, when the clan worshipped its totem they were effectively worshipping the clan because the clan contains the same emblem. The totem is a symbol of God *and* society.

Durkheim argued that the relationship between God and man was the same as the relationship between man and society. Man is seen as being dependent on God in the same way that man is dependent on society. While God is superior to man, so society is more important than the individual. God, states Durkheim, is a symbol for 'society'. In worshipping God, men are in fact worshipping society, and in doing so are constantly reminded of the individual's dependence on it.

Religious activity also served to unite the various clans together. The effects of religious ceremonies and activities was to reinforce shared ideas, values and ways of behaving without which society's moral order would begin to break down. By worshipping together people have a sense of commitment and belonging (what Durkheim terms 'collective conscience'), and individuals are united into a group with shared values. The result is that social solidarity is reinforced, deviant behaviour restrained and social change restricted because the existing social and moral order is sacred.

Durkheim believed all societies require the upholding and reaffirming of collective sentiments. While science may increasingly take over as a framework for understanding the world, various ceremonies and rituals will continually be required to unite groups together. This idea has been taken up by a number of sociologists who have explored the idea of a 'civil religion', in which various activities, while not overtly religious, serve to reaffirm the groups' values and collective conscience. The emotion, excitement and reverence of great civic occasions such as America's Thanksgiving and the Presidential Inaugurations, our own Silver Jubilee celebrations in 1977, or the Coronation, may serve to integrate and unite (see pages 75–81).

Analysis in these terms, however, has raised a number of different interpretations. While Shils and Young have offered one interpretation of the meaning of the Coronation, Birnbaum has subjected this to a Marxist critique. Some have argued that civil religion serves to tie the individual to society and allows for the expression and reaffirmation of the collective conscience, others have questioned the extent to which this is actually achieved. In part the interpretation of civil religion rests on assumptions about the nature of society.

The idea of religion being such a powerful and important integrating force in society has also been coupled with the secularisation debate. Those sociologists who see the process of secularisation well under way question how the moral order can be maintained in societies in which the traditional sources of this moral order, religious belief and practice, are being eroded.

While for some religion fulfills important integrative functions and the prospect of secularisation offers a bleak future, for others the picture is somewhat different. Although for both Durkheim and **Marx** (1818–1883), religion served to integrate society, Durkheim saw this as necessary for society to function, while Marx saw it as repressive. For Marx religion was essentially a tool of class exploitation and oppression. Those who are dominant in society require a means of disguising this exploitation – a set of justifications and beliefs which will mask, hide and legitimate the exploitative relationship between the haves and the have nots. Religion is important in this process since it suggests that the world is God-given and hence unchangeable. Consequently people are led away from any action which might change the existing structure and nature of society. At the same time religion serves to ease the pain of oppression by promising a paradise of eternal bliss after death. By promising salvation after death, by making a virtue out of suffering and by offering hope of supernatural intervention religion eases the pain of exploitation.

On a societal level Marx suggests that religion acts as a conservative force, justifying and legitimating present social arrangements. On an individual level religion also serves to hide man's true potential – it disguises the true nature of the world and man's ability to determine and shape it. By believing that God (which is man's construction) is all powerful, man's true nature, his true reality is hidden. Religion serves to hinder the development of true awareness (consciousness) and the realisation of man's power to create and control his social world. Thus 'the abolition of religion as the illusory happiness of men, is a demand for their real happiness.' (Marx, K., and Engels, F., *On Religion*, Moscow Foreign Languages Publishing House, 1955).

Religion and social change

Marx is often accused of being an 'economic determinist' because of the emphasis he gave to economic factors in shaping the nature of the social world. For him values and beliefs are essentially products of the economic structure and will justify and legitimate it. In this way religion will not be a source of social change. Max Weber is usually thought of as the sociologist who stressed the potential of beliefs and ideas in changing the social structure — religion could be seen as an agent of social change.

Both sociologists, I suggest, have been widely misinterpreted. While Marx stressed the role of economic factors in the formation of beliefs (including religion), and their subsequent justification of the existing order, he was aware of the complex inter-relationship between the economic base of society and ideas and beliefs. Although Marx never explicitly mentions this in his discussion of religion, it is implied in some of his other work, and is certainly a theme which has been developed by his followers.

Similarly, Weber has often been accused of a one-sided approach in which religion leads to social change — his argument concerning the role of Calvinism in the development of capitalism is usually referred to as evidence of this. Weber however was trying to redress an imbalance which he saw in Marx's writings; Weber's work is an attempt to show that ideas *can* influence the social structure. He was not saying that the connection was always in this direction. Weber, like Marx, was aware that religion was often used as a tool of justification; he talks not only of a religious explanation of disprivilege, but also of privilege.

For Weber man needs an explanation of suffering and destiny. Different religions provide these in different ways. The Hindu notion of Kharma in which transmigration of souls through a cycle compensates injustices in one life, or the Christian notion that such is God's grace and power that His acts are unintelligible to men and cannot be understood in human terms, are attempts to understand and make sense of human experiences. But Weber also argues that such explanations can have very important consequences for the way men behave. The notion of Kharma may produce resignation towards suffering while the notion of predestination may produce important consequences in terms of economic activity. Indeed Weber argued that Calvinist teachings (Calvinism was a particular brand of ascetic or frugal Protestantism), produced an attitude towards the world which was conducive to capitalist development. In other societies such as Oriental ones, although the potential for capitalist development in terms of the necessary material structure was present, the norms, values and ethics necessary for this development were not. Religious beliefs can therefore influence the nature and development of society.

Sectarian movements have also been studied in relation to the debate concerning social change. Thus Bryan Wilson argues that:

> Sects sometimes act as catalysts in history, crystallising in acute form the social discontents and aspirations, and marking the movements of social structural collapse, and sometimes heralding, or even promoting social integration.
>
> Wilson, 1970.

While some have argued that sectarian responses can lead to political awareness and social change, others have pointed to the conservative influence of such theories. Thus Eli Halevy explains the stability of English society during the social and economic upheavals of the eighteenth century by showing how discontented members of society came under the influence of Wesley and social and political unrest became substituted by religious fervour.

Such work has indicated that in some circumstances religion inhibits change and in others promotes it. More recent work has built on the foundations of earlier sociologists and begun to explore under which circumstances religion promotes and inhibits change. As Weber suggested, the nature of the religious beliefs and practices themselves may be a fruitful source of analysis. Other areas have included an exploration of the structure of religious organisations, the presence or absence of other

PART 2

Sociology and religion

2 The problem of definition

Religion presents the sociology student with considerable difficulties; difficulties which are most evident in this area, but are present in others. Clearly if we want to study an area of social life we need to be able to define and measure it. If we define the religious person as one who attends church regularly it may appear that we have a relatively easy gauge to assess a person's religious commitment, and that of society as a whole (even here problems exist, as we shall see later). If we use prayer as our index of religious commitment we have obvious problems of measurement. What is evident though is that our definition of religion will affect the tools we use to measure it, which in turn will affect the number and type of people we will assign as religious. As Stark and Glock note:

> The ambiguities in what religiousness can mean have led to serious failure in much research and writing on religious commitment. A good part of the recent dispute over whether American religion experienced a postwar revival or decline seems to have been produced by different observers adopting different definitions.
>
> Stark, R., and Glock C. Y., *American Piety: The Nature of Religious Commitment*, University of California Press, 1968.

Some obvious problems of definition and measurement can be seen in a few examples. Imagine that a close friend speaks vividly of how they saw the Virgin Mary, or witnessed someone 'speaking in tongues'. How do we assess, measure and explain such religious experiences? You see a friend coming out of church on a Sunday morning with their family – are they religious?

The classical sociologists were well aware of these difficulties and problems. Weber, for example, argued that:

> To define 'religion', to say what it is, is not possible at the start of a presentation. . . Definition can be attempted, if at all, only at the conclusion of the study.
>
> Weber, M., *The Sociology of Religion,* Methuen, London, 1965.

Although Weber's work gave some indication of how he defined religion, it is difficult to conceive of how an analysis of something can take place without identifying what it is to be analysed. Although definitions may be problematic, and we may wish to adapt them after study, we nevertheless need to begin with one.

Perhaps the most famous definition of religion is that of **Emile Durkheim** who argued that one characteristic of religious beliefs is that they classify all things into two groups, the sacred and the profane, the religious and the secular. Sacred things might include gods or spirits, rocks or pebbles, pieces of wood – literally anything can be sacred. Such sacred things are usually considered superior in both their dignity and power, and are also accompanied by a set of ritual practices and ceremonies which separate them from the profane. Because these two groups are always separated in man's thoughts it is easy to recognise this classification.

This distinction between the sacred and the profane provided the basis for his definition of religion. However, the sacred also served to bind people together into a moral unity which Durkheim called a church. Thus he arrived at his final definition of religion:

> a unified system of beliefs and practices relative to sacred things, that is to say things set apart and forbidden – beliefs and practices which unite into one moral unity called a church, all those who adhere to them.
>
> Durkheim, E., *The Elementary Forms of the Religious Life,*
> Free Press, New York, 1965.

Durkheim's interest in religion was in those aspects which had a social function and as such he was not concerned with more private elements of religious experience. Furthermore, since in many contemporary societies evidence suggests that there may be little connection between religious belief and practice, the appropriateness of this definition must be questioned. Thus while in some societies there appear to be high rates of religious belief and low rates of religious activity such as church attendance, in others such as the United States there appear to be relatively high rates of church attendance coupled with lower rates of religious belief.

In the face of considerable controversy and uncertainty over what is meant by the term 'religious', Glock and Stark have developed a number of 'core dimensions' of religiousness. They argue that many definitions of religion have failed to effectively come to terms with a phenomenon which manifests itself in many different ways – the religious beliefs and practices within Christian churches vary considerably, and certainly between religious groups such as Jews, Moslems and Hindus. One way to define religion which can take account of this diversity is by developing a series of 'core dimensions' of religiousness. These core dimensions comprise belief, practice, experience, knowledge and consequences.

The belief dimension acknowledges that a religious person will hold a certain outlook and will accept the major beliefs of any given religion. Amongst Christians such beliefs may include the Virgin Birth, the Resurrection, and the Ascension.

Religion also implies certain practices by which people show and practice their commitment. Such activities may include various acts of formal worship such as taking communion and confirmation, as well as the more informal and usually private activities of individual prayer and reading from sacred books such as the Bible and Quran.

The experience dimension takes into account that religions tend to have expectations concerning a direct experience with some supernatural force. It is concerned with:

> those feelings, perceptions, and sensations, which are experienced by an actor or defined by a religious groups as involving some communication, however slight, with a divine essence, that is, with God, with ultimate reality, with transcendental authority.
>
> Stark and Glock, 1968.

A religious person is also expected to possess a degree of information and understanding of the basis of the religion – the

knowledge dimension. While there is a clear relationship between belief and knowledge, Glock and Stark argue that the two
dimensions are separate since a person's knowledge does not
always lead to belief. Similarly, religious beliefs may rest on very
little knowledge and understanding.

That such beliefs, practices, experiences and knowledge are
likely to affect behaviour is illustrated by their consequence
dimension. Religious people are expected to act and think
differently.

While the authors argue that these five 'core dimensions' are
related, being religious in one dimension does not imply being
religious in another. Thus holding religious beliefs may not
necessarily lead to religious practices or experience. However,
while some religions put more emphasis on particular aspects of
the 'core dimensions', Glock and Stark argue that all are important elements of religiosity.

Glock and Stark's 'core dimensions' help us to identify the
major features of a religion we are still left with the difficulties of
operationalising (i.e. put into a form which can be measured) the
dimensions that they outline, and especially with accurately
measuring and taking account of the meanings which lie behind
them. Although it may be possible to measure the extent of
religious practices such as taking communion, church weddings
and the like, the significance of these is more difficult to gauge.
Is someone who marries in a registry office less religious than
one who marries in church?

While many sociologists have attempted to define the religious in terms of some belief in supernatural forces which affect
man, others have argued that such a view is rather narrow. They
claim that the sociology of religion should not limit itself to
studying what has traditionally been seen as its field of inquiry,
but should explore 'belief systems' generally. These include the
different ways people interpret the world and the explanatory
frameworks they use. As such, the sociology of religion becomes
a part of the sociology of knowledge – the way people interpret,
make sense of, and give meaning to the world around them. This
approach is especially connected with the work of Berger and
Luckmann.

Berger and Luckmann are very critical of much contemporary
research on religion which they claim has been carried out under
the support and encouragement of the established churches.

Much of the research they suggest has been a 'religious variety of market research'. As such the sociology of religion has tended to be defined in ecclesiastical terms i.e. it has tended to focus on churches – church attendances, marriages and the like.

For Berger and Luckmann sociologists should be concerned with the way people make sense of the world around them. An individual's knowledge of the world is a social construct which is continually reinforced and legitimated. Religion has, and continues to play an important part in both constructing and legitimating man's 'universe of meaning'. If this position is accepted then the sociology of religion becomes concerned with much broader issues than previously. It begins to analyse the various forms of knowledge about the world which are available, the ways in which such knowledge is acquired, and the various organisations which distribute such knowledge.

The definition of religion which Berger and Luckmann adopt can be labelled an 'inclusive' one – religion becomes the way in which man attempts to formulate an all-embracing system of meaning, and as such Marxism might be seen as a religion. If, as many have argued, this attempt to make sense of the world and give meaning to it is a necessary and inevitable feature of mankind then in this respect we will always be religious. However, there is a difficulty here since not only would many Marxists reject a religious label, but many would suggest that there is considerable difference between this and 'conventionally and intuitively understood religion'. (Robertson, R., *The Sociological Interpretation of Religion*, Blackwell, Oxford, 1970).

If, on the other hand, we employ an 'exclusive' definition of religion (one which excludes meaning systems such as Marxism), then we may be forced to rule out of our analysis those meaning systems which may both be of interest to us, and be related to those beliefs which Robertson labels 'obviously religious'. One of the great difficulties which has faced those studying religion is that sociologists who have claimed to be discussing religion have in fact been talking about different things. For this reason it seems worthwhile to consider religion as one sort of meaning system, but to be aware that not all meaning systems are religious. For this reason the definition of religion adopted here will be based on that by Worsley: *a set of beliefs which in some way refers to, and looks for validation in, a dimension beyond the empirical–technical realm.* While, like all definitions of religion, this is open to criticism, it does provide a starting point.

Before turning our attention to a number of themes and issues connected with religion, it is important to make a distinction between a number of types of religious organisations: church, denomination and sect.

A church is usually, defined as a stable, formal organisation with a hierarchy of paid officials. It is generally integrated with the wider economic and social structure and has a set of beliefs and values which are widely accepted. Worship tends to be formal, and although all sections of the population are represented, the higher status groups tend to be over-represented. A good example is the Church of England which is formally connected with the State and Monarchy.

A denomination is a religious organisation which accepts and is accepted by the wider society, but does not usually have any formal connection with the State. Worship may be less formal than a church, and its general relationship to other churches and denominations is one of coexistance and acceptance. Examples of denominations are Methodists and the United Reformed Church.

Sects are generally smaller organisations which tend to be insular and reject the values of the wider society, often being in conflict with it. There is often an absence of paid officials and, as a consequence, there is a tendency for the services to be informal and for members to be responsible for different aspects of the organisation. Members often come from the lower status groups. Their teachings frequently demand intense commitment and loyalty from members and they are often intolerant of others, believing that only by following their teachings can salvation or enlightenment be achieved. Examples of sects include the Mormons and Jehovah's Witnesses.

3 Secularisation

One of the major debates in the sociology of religion has been concerned with the extent to which modern industrial societies can be described as 'secular' – the extent to which religion can be seen to be losing social significance. The major difficulty with the secularisation thesis is that in the same way as there is no widespread acceptance of what 'religious' means, so too there is no general agreement over the term 'secularisation'.

Bryan Wilson, one of the major proponents of the thesis, defined secularisation as 'the process whereby religious thinking, practices and institutions lose social significance'. (Wilson, B. R., *Religion in Secular Society*, Watts, London, 1966). He does not mean to imply that all members of society have a 'secularised consciousness' or that people no longer have an interest in religion. His main concern is over the way that religion has ceased to have any significance for the working of the social system (see Reading 7).

Like other definitions, Wilson's contains a number of difficulties and problems, and rests on various assumptions. While some have viewed the term as a form of counter religious ideology, others have tended to assume that secularisation is self-evident and what is required is an attempt to explain the processes by which it occurs. One difficulty of Wilson's definition concerns what social significance means and how we can assess and measure it. What would be an index of loss of significance? Can we use the number of paintings with a 'secular' as opposed to a 'religious' theme as an indicator? Furthermore, many definitions of secularisation tend to assume that historically life was more 'religious', or at least less secular than it is today. This presumes that we can gauge the influence of religion in the past. Although Wilson claims that this assumption is perfectly legitimate, others have questioned it.

Such are the problems and ambiguities surrounding the concept that some have argued that we should abandon the term. While there clearly are difficulties, there is no doubt that the concept has stimulated much research and debate, and although a clear and generally accepted definition of secularisation would be advantageous, its present ambiguity has served to draw together a wide range of diverse and interesting material. In the following section we shall explore the different areas sociologists have looked into when analysing secularisation and examine the areas of controversy and debate.

Secularisation: areas of controversy

Decline in church membership and participation

A number of sociologists have pointed to a wide range of statistical material which for them indicates secularising trends. Using a variety of sources and indices such as church attendance and membership, baptisms, confirmations, marriages and the number of clergy, they have sought to prove that secularisation is occurring. However, while such statistics do appear to indicate a decline in these indices of religion (see Figures 7.1, 7.2 and 7.3, pages 67–69), they, like other social statistics, need to be treated with caution. Various intepretations and problems have been outlined:

1 D. Martin, for example, points to a number of difficulties with such figures. He notes that they must always be seen in their 'demographic context', since changes in the age distribution of the population may be significant.

Furthermore, many of these statistics are collected by the organisations themselves and may not be directly comparable. Thus, for example, criteria for membership may vary both between and within churches – is a member of the Church of England someone who, when asked when church they belong to, replies 'C. of E.', or is it someone who is on the electoral roll, or else attends regularly? Not only have methods of church statistics varied over time (for example, since 1978 figures for infant baptism in the Church of England have been based on baptisms of those under one year of age, and may not be comparable with previous years), but the apparent decline of church attendance on a Sunday may simply reflect that less people attend twice, not that the total number has declined.

Some of the statistics may also be inaccurate since increased geographical mobility may mean that some people are counted as members of two churches. A tendency to attend one church one week and another the next might also produce errors.

2 While some interpret religious statistics as a sign of decline, others from a different perspective point to the continued widespread routine of church attendance. Thus Martin argues that:

in the course of a year one out of every two Britons will have entered a church, not for an event in the life cycle, or for a special personal or civic occasion, but for a service within the ordinary pattern of institutional religion.

Martin, D., *A Sociology of English Religion*, Heinemann, London, 1967.

If we include the 'hatching, matching and dispatching' events, the proportion attending would be significantly higher.

3 Despite these difficulties of accuracy and interpretation of church statistics, it is widely accepted that there has been a reduction in factors such as church attendance, at least in this country. However, it is a significant step to imply that this signifies secularisation. Because a person attends church, does this mean that they are religious, and similarly, does a decline in religious participation indicate a decline in religious belief? Various social surveys have consistently revealed that large number of people have some form of religious belief (see Figure 7.6, page 72). While a recent Gallup Poll showed that 76 per cent of this country claim to believe in God, the figure for America is higher at around 94 per cent. Such figures not only point to the difficulties in assuming that attendance figures etc., indicate a lack of religious faith, they also point to the difficulty of making generalisations concerning all modern industrial societies.

A 1983 survey by Gallup commissioned by the Bible Society showed that when asked their religious affiliation, 64 per cent considered themselves Church of England, 11 per cent Roman Catholic, 7 per cent Methodist, 2 per cent Baptist and the remainder either 'other' or no religion (see Figure 7.5, page 71). Clearly, such figures need interpreting carefully and may not tell us a great deal about qualitative differences in belief. Although figures such as the percentage of people expressing a belief in

God or religious affiliation do not tell us about the meaning of these or how it affects their personal lives, they do perhaps indicate the continuing social importance attached to such beliefs and affiliations.

4 Demerath and Hammond explain the problems of assuming that attendance and belief can be equated. They point to the fact that even if the statistics were beyond criticism, there remains the problem of intepretation:

> we should avoid the quick assumption that church members are always highly religious in their personal beliefs and activities, or that church non-members are otherwise irreligious.
>
> > Demerath, N. J., and Hammond, P. E., *Religion in Social Context,* Random House, New York, 1969.

Despite a relationship between church membership and attendance and social class, there is a negative relationship between class and other measures of religiosity such as belief. People of higher status may feel obliged to attend church in order to maintain a certain social status.

5 Coupled with the point above is the assumption that higher figures of attendance in the past indicate a higher level of religiosity. Such figures may indicate that in the past different values were attached to Sunday attendances. Furthermore, although figures on attendance, etc., were collected, little indication of the extent of religious beliefs and the meanings these had are available. While for some the past represents a golden age of religiosity, others are far more sceptical.

6 Another way of explaining the statistics is to look at the popular perception of religious decline. Thus a 1979 Gallup Poll Commissioned by the European Values System Study Group, showed that although 48 per cent of the sample said that the first Commandment applied fully to themselves ('I am the Lord your God. You should have no other God before me.'), only 18 per cent believed that others accepted it (see Figures 7.7 and 7.8, pages 72 and 73).

7 Statistical evidence for secularisation is far from universal. Statistics for the United States show an apparent growth in the number of people belonging to and regularly attending churches. Such figures however again have to be treated with caution

and may reflect an increase in the number of denominations reporting their attendance figures, changing definitions of church membership, etc. As we have also seen, such figures tell us little about the meaning beyond them – it may not be that Americans are more 'religious' but that church attendance has a different meaning for them.

8 Although there is some evidence that membership, attendance and various religious activities such as weddings and baptisms connected with the established church have declined, there has been a considerable growth in other areas. While the overall numbers of religious groups such as the Jehovah's Witnesses, Mormons and Krishna Consciousness remain small, they have experienced significant growth in recent years.

Given that many of these groups make greater demands upon their members than most established churches, some have argued that the growth of these movements marks a trend not towards secularisation, but an increasing interest and concern for the 'sacred'.

From the analysis so far, it should be evident that a decline in church related activities (assuming this is accurate), does not necessarily provide evidence of secularisation. While the claims, counter claims and different interpretations may leave many somewhat bewildered and uncertain, they do serve to remind us of the difficulty of analysing religious factors and the complexity of the secularisation debate. The debate becomes more complex when we begin to explore other areas of controversy.

Religious disengagement

Another index of secularisation which has been used is that of the disengagement of the Church from wider society. The Church is seen as relinquising its influence on other spheres of activity. Those who argue that this process is occurring point to the decline of the Church in terms of its power, control and influence over every aspect of human activity and the growth of specialised agencies which have taken over many of the activities which were previously the domain of religious bodies.

In the Middle Ages, the Church was more openly involved in a wide range of activities. During such times, not only was there a very close connection between Church and rulers, but the

Church had considerable influence over areas such as social control. There existed informal controls such as confession and the fear of Divine intervention, as well as more formal mechanisms, such as church courts. Religious bodies were largely responsible for education and for social welfare provision.

Today, however, despite having some influence in education such as church schools and religious education (and even here their power is limited), the control over these activities has increasingly been given to secular bodies such as Local Education Authorities. In areas of law and social welfare other specialised agencies directed by the State have taken over. The activities of the churches are now rather more limited to spiritual concerns, and to those important events in the life cycle – 'hatching, matching and dispatching.' This type of argument, as Hill points out is similar to the one which has been made concerning the family in modern industrial societies:

> Just as the multifunctional 'traditional' family (providing among other things governmental, religious, educational and economic services for its members) is seen as having been stripped of such non-essential functions and – according to some commentators – is thereby in a state of decay, so the traditional religious institutions which at one time were responsible for educational and welfare functions have been relieved of these activities by state agencies and – or so the secularisation argument goes – find themselves more and more in a marginal position in industrial societies.
>
> Hill, 1973.

Similar criticisms which have been made concerning the loss of function argument in the case of the family, can also be seen in the case of the disengagement of the Church from wider society. A number of criticisms have been made of the assumptions behind this measure of secularisation.

1 It is clear that the Church continues to involve itself with, and have some influence over, what could be described as secular concerns. The Church has involved itself, for example, with inequality, nuclear weapons and euthanasia. Organisations such as the Salvation Army have remained very actively concerned with the homeless and destitute, and while there may have been some erosion in their influence in comparison with the past, the

Church has far from completely divorced itself from such concerns.

2 A number of writers have questioned the extend to which the Church of the past can be seen to represent a truly religious phenomenon. They point to corruption, concern with its own material well being and search for power and influence, rather than its interest with the spiritual needs of the population. In this way, its limitation to obviously religious concerns may indicate a more genuinely religious phenomenon in comparison with the past.

3 Talcott Parsons also criticises the argument that the Church's disengagement from wider society can be seen as evidence of a decline in its importance. According to Parsons, in a society which is highly differentiated, religious institutions may become more specialised, but this does not mean less important. Although religious institutions may no longer have a direct influence over areas such as education and politics, they do have an influence in terms of the religious norms and values followed by individuals. The values and attitudes of those who are active in the religious sphere influence their activities in the secular realm. As Parsons argues, the influence of the Church is not directly:

> through organisational jurisdiction over certain aspects of life now structurally differentiated from them, but through the value–commitments and motivational commitments of individuals.
>
> Parsons, T., *Social Structure and Personality*, Collier Macmillan, London, 1970.

The rationalisation of the world

A number of writers have argued that the process of secularisation is closely linked to the growth of 'rational' and 'scientific' thought. One of the consequences of this development is the decline in religious explanations of the world – the world becomes deprived of its sacred character. Many of the ideas associated with this type of argument can be seen to have their origins in the work of classical sociologist such as Weber and anthropologists such as Malinowski.

Whereas many of Malinowski's contemporaries tended to have an evolutionary view of man and religion in which magic becomes superceded by religion and in turn religion by science, he maintained that religion and magic in all societies served to ease emotional stress and anxiety. Even though the Trobriand Islanders studied by Malinowski had considerable knowledge about gardening and employed rational procedures, these were never completely adequate to explain why their crops sometimes failed. In a society full of danger and uncertainty and in which there was a continual threat of injury, disease and death, there was always an element of the inexplicable, the 'unknowable'. Religion and magic served to offer an explanation of the events for which other frameworks could not account.

Weber, however, appeared to suggest that religious explanations would gradually be taken over by 'scientific' rational ones. One of the key characteristics of modern society, according to Weber, is its emphasis on a rationalised economy and a rational mentality. Society is governed by decisions based on careful evaluation of costs and benefits, a greater openness towards change and a flexible approach. Although this approach to the world signalled the erosion of religion, religion itself was a necessary agent of its development – hence the importance Weber attached to Calvinism in establishing the Capitalist spirit (see pages 41–43). Once this rationality was established, it become divorced from its origins and was carried forward by its own momentum. The trend which Weber identified can usefully be illustrated by a recent quote from the founder of the MacDonalds hamburger chain: 'I speak of faith in MacDonalds as if it were a religion. I believe in God, family and MacDonalds – and in the office that order is reversed.' While religion may still play a part in a person's life, it may no longer be the guiding principle affecting all areas of social activity.

One of the effects of rationalisation is that religious explanations and beliefs begin to lose social significance. Weber talks about the progressive 'disenchantment of the world' in which the supernatural is no longer significant. Phenomena which were previously explained in terms of miracles and the supernatural are now open to scientific explanations, and the dominant view comes to be one in which all occurrences can be explained by this rational framework. Although he appears to suggest that bureaucratic organisation and rationalism are inevitable, he also presents us with a picture of somewhat aimless individuals trying to make sense of their lives without the framework of religious beliefs.

While in the past agriculture may have been carried out in a traditional way and various rituals performed to ensure productivity, today consideration is given to cost-benefit analysis, careful calculation of fertiliser and pesticides and a general willingness to employ scientific techniques to ensure maximum output. Problems of drought or flood are no longer solved by prayer or ritual, but by irrigation and drainage schemes. Religious explanation and belief are increasingly seen as irrelevant to many areas of social life.

Sociologists such as **Wilson** have argued that this progressive movement towards 'rationalisation' and 'desacralisation' has effectively undermined religious belief and influence. In this way, scientific explanations have attacked various aspects of the Christian faith – the continual debates over the origins of man, for example, beginning with Darwin's evolutionary theory, have thrown supporters of the creationist theory on the defensive. Similarly, technology itself is governed by rational efficiency. With the increasing use of computers and other devices of applied science, people are made more and more aware of the importance of rationality with a subsequent decline in religious belief. Increasingly, rational explanations are taken as the serious ones, and religious explanations thought of as naïve. As a consequence, it could be argued that while scientists have risen in status, holders of religious knowledge have not.

While Wilson's arguments have a ring of truth to them, we should not fall into the trap of assuming that here again we have evidence of secularisation. While there may have been a growth of rational and scientific ways of thinking and behaving, we should be cautious of adopting an over–rationalised view of contemporary society. A number of reservations have been put forward concerning the type of argument presented by Wilson:

1 There is a danger of assuming that in the past 'primitive' belief systems were not 'rational'. A number of writers, however, have suggested that many 'religious' belief systems bear a number of similarities to 'scientific' ones, in the sense that they are both attempts to explain cause and effect. Marvin Harris argues that many of the apparently irrational religious beliefs and practices

have a very rational and practical basis. He suggests that the Hindu veneration of cows can be explained in terms of their importance to life – they are an economically viable source of traction, fuel, fertilizer, milk, floor covering, meat and leather. (Harris, M., *Cows, Pigs, Wars and Witches*, Hutchinson and Co., 1975).

2 While science has contributed to our understanding, it has not replaced religious beliefs. As we have seen, a high percentage of the population in modern industrial societies claim to have some belief in God. Furthermore, if we look at the number of people who believe in superstitious rituals such as touching wood, or throwing salt, and those who strongly believe in astrology, fortune telling, ghosts and premonitions, it is clear that the scientific/rational realm does not reign completely (Reading 1).

3 It may be that while science is capable of explanation at one level, at another, things are still regarded as inexplicable. While Western medicine may explain birth and death in terms of physiological and biological factors, religion is often used to explain the ultimate meaning of these events – why some people die in accidents, or when young, etc. It may be that in Malinowski's terms people still turn to religion when attempting to cope with the anxiety, stress and uncertainty of life.

Religious pluralism

A number of writers such as Bryan Wilson have argued that historically religions were monolithic, i.e. there existed one dominant faith, one world view. Religions had a monopoly and tended to administer to a whole society. Alternatives were either absorbed, segregated or suppressed.

Society today, however, is not characterised by one single religious faith, but by a plurality of different religions. While some agree that the wide variety of religious organisations is evidence of pluralism, others extend this definition and use it to refer to 'universes of meaning'. Hence now 'science' or 'Marxism' may provide competing world views.

In a world characterised by a wide range of religious views, their power and influence becomes weaker. The competition between them means that their credibility is undermined and they can no longer take for granted the allegiance of their members. One of the consequences of this is that religious views, which at one time could be imposed, now have to be marketed and sold to potential consumers. As Peter Berger notes: ' the religious institutions become marketing agencies and the religious traditions become consumer commodities.' (Berger, P. L., *The Social Reality of Religion,* Faber & Faber, London, 1969). A further consequence of this development from religious monopolies to competing marketing agencies is that they begin to organise themselves in ways which reflect this competitive situation There is a tendency not only towards an increased bureaucratic and rational structure, but also towards collaboration. Open competition between different agencies becomes irrational because the costs may cancel out any potential gains – competition between groups may not be good for the public image. While, from a sociological perspective, the ecumenical movement might be interpreted in this way, and as evidence of the weakening hold of religion, we should remember that those engaged in the movement may interpret in a very different way.

The growth of sects has also been utilised in the argument concerning religious pluralism. The only way to experience a truly religious way of life is to isolate oneself from the secular world. For Wilson sects are a consequence of increased secularisation and the decline of traditional religion; they are a confirmation of the secularisation process, but can do nothing to halt its progress (see Reading 23).

Others however, while accepting the arguments concerning the development of religious pluralism, interpret it somewhat differently.

1 The growth and development of a plurality of religious organisations points to the continued vitality of religion and a need for it. Religious organisations are attempting to meet the differing needs which people have, and while this may mean that religion is in a state of change, this is different from saying that it is in a state of decline.

2 While writers such as Wilson see sects as evidence of secularisation, others see them in terms of a religious revival. Andrew Greeley, for example, sees the growth of new religious movements on University campuses as a process of 'resacralisation'. The sacred realm has been re-established (Greeley, A. M., *The Persistance of Religion*, S.C.M. Press, London, 1973).

In a somewhat different light, Glock and Bellah see the new religious movements as an indication of a new awareness, an increased spiritual sensitivity and a search for meaning. They see one possible consequence of these groups as bringing about a 'new alternative' to contemporary society – a movement towards the 'quest for ultimate reality'. (Glock and Bellah, 1976).

The secularisation of religious institutions

In a timely warning about making generalisations concerning secularisation Wilson warns us that 'patterns in which it is manifested are culturally and historically specific.' (Wilson, 1982). One example of this appears to be the extend to which secularising tendencies can be seen within the Church itself. Thus in America it is often claimed that although religious institutions appear to thrive and attendances are high, these organisations have tended to abandon their religious aims and have become involved in numerous other activities which can only loosely be called 'religious' – 'other-worldly' motivations have been replaced by 'this-worldly' concerns. This difference between America and England has been summarised by **Scharf**:

> In America there is secularisation within the churches; in England there is secularisation by withdrawal from the churches, with the members who remain being 'truly' religious.
>
> Scharf, 1970.

One explanation of this difference has been provided by **Herberg** who argues that it can be related to social and geographical mobility in which the Church provided a focus for community life. In Britain, in which there was a more settled communal life, there was never a need for the Church to become a community agency.

Herberg begins his explanation with a definition of 'authentic religion':

> an emphasis on the supernatural, a deep inner conviction of the reality of supernatural power, a serious commitment to religious teachings, a strong element of theological doctrine and a refusal to compromise religious beliefs and values with those of wider society.
>
> Herberg, W., *Protestant, Catholic, Jew,*
> Doubleday, New York, 1955.

He argues that the major religious organisations in the United States have failed to live up to this definition and have largely accommodated their theology to fit the American way of life. Herberg identifies three factors which have led to the wide variety of religious groups in America. Firstly, the effects of large scale immigration which created the need for a sense of identity and community. The various denominations provided this and many are still identified with particular ethnic groups. Secondly, the idea of equality of opportunity and freedom before the law which enabled a wide variety of religious groups to develop. Thirdly, the absence of any established church to hinder the formation of these new religious organisations.

Increasingly the newcomers began to identify with the American way of life. The need to feel a sense of belonging meant that these religious communities began to stress those values which were common to all and which enabled a person to identify themselves as American. By belonging to a church, not only were you provided with a sense of identity and the warmth of a close, secure community, but you were also demonstrating your commitment to everything America stands for.

American churches are seen by Herberg as echoing the American Dream. They stand for democracy and freedom, success and attainment. For Herberg religion in America especially, has little to do with 'authentic religion' and is further evidence of secularisation. In America membership of a religious organisation means something different. As Scharf notes:

> being American includes being religious, and finding in religion a sanction for the American values of individualism, activism, efficiency and self-improvement.
>
> Scharf, 1970.

While Herberg's views have been supported by Wilson, they are not without criticism. It is questionable, for example, whether Americans share the same attitudes – does a broad value consensus exist over what America stands for? Secondly, Herberg's thesis implies that in Britain there is less need for religious communities, but with increased geographical mobility and the formation of 'new towns' we might predict an increased need for the type of religious community identified in the United States. It is questionable whether there is any evidence for this occurring.

On the question of whether these trends identified by Herberg indicate secularisation, some have argued that rather than 'selling out', religious organisations have adapted themselves to the needs of their members. Furthermore, as Scharf argues:

> Provided the believer connects these worldly values with a divine power who is looked up to as the sanction or protector of them, and whose relation to mankind requires ritual celebration, they should surely be recognised as religious values.
>
> Scharf, 1970.

Religious decline or transformation?

While some sociologists have seen evidence of secularisation in factors such as declining church attendance, the rationalisation of the world, the disengagement of the Church from wider society, and religious pluralism, others have argued that this does not indicate a decline in religion, but a transformation of it. Berger and Luckmann are major proponents of this transformmation view.

In a series of influential writings they have suggested that institutional religion is only one form of religion, and while this may be in decline, religion itself is not.

Luckmann argues that definitions of religion and secularisation have been tied to institutional religion. One of the consequences of this is that research tends to be carried out in these terms – indexes of religiosity are connected with the churches. For Luckmann this is only one type of religion, and one which is peripheral to modern society, although he is aware that to treat religion this way requires a broader definition of it. Hence he refers to symbolic 'universe of meaning' by which men make sense of and interpret their experiences. Selecting from a wide range of sources men construct their own personal meaning systems – their own 'sacred cosmos' by which human experience is ultimately meaningful. Religion becomes private and largely invisible from the prying eyes of the sociologist.

Berger arrives at a similar conclusion arguing that religion 'is the human enterprise by which a sacred cosmos is established' (Berger, 1969). This is important for maintaining a meaningful model of the world. If religion is defined in terms of religious institutions he argues that secularisation has occurred. The development of a distinct institutionalised religion means that it becomes segregated from other areas of social activity. With the growth of pluralism in the area of religious belief, institutionalised religion has difficulty in maintaining a monopoly. There comes into being a wide range of meaning systems by which men can interpret the world. Religion becomes pluralistic and privatised, and a matter of individual choice – men construct their own religious meaning systems.

Both Berger and Luckmann are suggesting that religion, when defined as any meaning system by which men interpret the world, is alive and well; indeed it is an indispensible element of human existence. While in the past these meaning systems were largely derived from a monolithic institutionalised religious form, today a wide variety of sources are available. This implies that the study of religion needs to be able to analyse individual structures of personal meaning, something which is methodologically complex, and which requires far more than analysing trends in church attendance.

A somewhat different picture is provided by Bellah although he also argues that what we are witnessing is a transformation rather than a decline in religious belief and activity. Defining religion as 'a set of symbolic forms and acts which relate man to the ultimate conditions of his environment' (Bellah, R. N., 'Religious Evolution', *American Sociological Review*, 1964) he outlines five stages of religious development: primitive, archaic, historic, early modern and modern. In the modern type he, like Berger and Luckmann, sees an increasing variety of religious symbols from which people can choose. Rather than interpreting such trends as secularisation Bellah sees them as signs of the increasing acceptance that the individual must work out his own ultimate solutions to life.

To this general idea of transformation we can add the ideas of Parsons. As we have previously noted, Parsons argues that the role of religion has been redefined. While religion may have lost some of its peripheral functions, its basic function of maintaining the commitment of the individual to society remains. If this is the case then we might expect that religious institutions would have a clearer role in society and be separated from secular realms. Whether this has occurred is debatable.

Conclusion

Some sociologists have argued that religion is in decline; others have argued that it is merely going through a transformation. In part this debate hinges on different interpretations of various phenomena, but it also hinges on the definition of religion. Those who define religion in broad terms such as the formation of universes of meaning are using an 'inclusive' definition. Thus communism, rationalism, humanism and various other 'isms' come under the category of religion since they are attempts to formulate universes of meaning. On the other hand, those definitions which are 'exclusive' and are concerned with those activities which are 'obviously religious', may see recent changes as evidence of decline (Readings 10 and 11).

Whatever definition of religion is adopted, and despite the debate over its transformation or decline, there is general agreement that religion in contemporary Western society has changed. A number of factors have been put forward to explain this: some have argued that religion contained the seeds of change; others that there is an evolutionary pattern to religion; others have pointed to the growth in bureaucracy, science and rationality and the State. What is important however, is to see religion and the debates which surround it in a broader context than is often referred to. There is a danger of exploring the secularisation debate and after trying to come to terms with its various complexities, saying 'So what?'.

In part I suspect that this is a consequence of the sociology of religion being embedded in what has been called 'ecclesiastical market research'. This is far removed from Weber's concern with religion as an important agent of social change, or Durkheim's view of religion as an agent of societal integration and stability. However, it is possible to see the secularisation debate as of central interest to sociology, and not as something peripheral and relatively unimportant. Although in the following paragraphs I shall use only one example, it does serve to place the debate in a broader context and show its importance and possible implications.

For Bryan Wilson various changes in religion, which he intreprets as secularisation, occur as social life is transformed from one that is communally based to one that is society based. He argues that the process of societalisation (by which he means 'the process by which large scale, ongoing, internally coordinated, complex systems are established, usually including, as a significant element, the process of state formation' (Wilson, 1982)), necessarily results in religious institutions losing social significance. Whereas in the community religion served to maintain the social order, was a source of social knowledge and was at the very heart of community life, this is no longer the case. In the past religion was a very important element in maintaining society, and provided the very foundations upon which society was based.

Now this leads to an obvious problem; if religious institutions are in a state of progressive decline what is the consequence? For Wilson the breakdown of commmunity and decline of religion will lead to increased social disorder. Thus he speaks of the:

> growth of crime, of vandalism, and of neurosis and mental breakdown; the growing disruption of marriage; the increase of various types of addiction, whether to drugs, alcohol, or gambling; the incidence of personal isolation, loneliness and suicide.

> Wilson, 1982.

Britain is characterised by strikes and absenteeism, vandalism and hooliganism (see Reading 8).

While such a view may have wide appeal, and although Wilson is to be applauded for linking secularisation with the broader concerns characteristic of the classical sociologist, his analysis does contain difficulties. Two such difficulties will serve to illustrate the problems of accepting Wilson's theory at face value. First of all there is the assumption that religious institutions have declined, and the absence of any detailed historical perspective. The decline of religion and erosion of community which Wilson refers to are presumably lengthy processes, so why are we only now witnessing the consequences? Secondly there is the assumption that the instances of social disorder which he refers to (and here we could question the extent and significance of them), are a consequence of a decline in religion. There is a danger that having assumed secularisation has occurred and that this will produce difficulties, he searches for evidence of this and finds it. A more detailed analysis of the causes of industrial conflict or marriage breakdown may well produce different interpretations and contributing factors.

4 Religion and social change

The analysis of the relation between religion and social change has usually been couched in terms of a debate between Marx and Weber. Marx is usually credit with the idea that religion will justify and legitimate the existing social order, and so inhibit change, while Weber is usually thought of as suggesting that religion can cause social change. Both writers have been widely misinterpreted, partly due to the values and preferences of various commentators, but also because their writings on religion were taken out of context and not located within their broader theoretical frameworks.

In this chapter we shall analyse the ideas of Marx and Weber and also look at other work which seeks to examine the complex relationship between religion and social change. As we shall see, in some cases religion promotes change and in others hinders it. One of our aims will be to explore those factors which might account for religion being change inducing or change inhibiting.

Religion as change inhibiting

Marx believed that God did not create mankind, but rather mankind created God, just as mankind created wage labour and 'democracy', etc. In 'primitive' societies religious explanations were used to come to terms with phenomena which were beyond understanding, but gradually these beliefs and explanations became justifications and legitimations for keeping society as it was. Thus, for example, in the sixteenth and seventeenth centuries, the idea of a 'Great chain of being' existed in which the social hierarchy of God, kings, bishops, lords, freemen and serfs was argued to be natural and God given. Similarly in the eighteenth and nineteenth centuries many people thought it was largely senseless to try to do anything about poverty since it was God who had created the rich and the poor, and it was therefore immoral and ungodly to try to change things. Religious justifications have also been used to legitimate social inequality and status inequality such as the Indian caste system.

It is clear that if society changes those who are particularly privileged probably have most to lose. Thus for Marxists, religion is particularly important to this group. Not only will it serve to justify their position, but it will serve to hide or disguise the real basis of their power and hinder the development of any awareness and understanding on the part of those who are at the bottom of the social ladder. How is this group able to do this?

For Marx the basis of power lies in owning and controlling the forces of production i.e. the technology, resources, raw materials and knowledge used in the process of production. In feudal societies this consisted of owning and controlling land, while in capitalist societies it consists of the ownership of factories and so forth. Such ownership not only gave control of the production of goods and services, but also over the production and distribution of ideas:

> The ideas of the ruling class are, in every age, the ruling ideas i.e. the class which is the dominant material force in society is at the same time its dominant intellectual force. The class which has the means of material production at its disposal, has control at the same time over the means of mental production.
>
> Marx, K. and Engels, F., *The German Ideology,*
> Lawrence and Wishart, 1974.

Thus the dominant ideas present at any particular time reflect the interests of the powerful.

Marx believed that history was divided into a number of time periods or epochs, each characterised by a particular mode of production e.g. in primitive societies hunting and gathering, and in feudal societies settled agriculture. The change from a feudal society based on agriculture to a capitalist society based on industrial production occurred mainly because of the development of new means of production such as steam power and the factory system.

This change was not an easy transition, partly because of the struggle between the rising bourgeoisie and the declining feudal aristocracy. One dimension of this struggle was in the area of ideas about the nature of man and society i.e. it concerned belief systems or 'ideologies'. The ideology of the feudal aristocracy placed great emphasis on the idea of tradition and on doing things the way they have always been done. That of the rising bourgeoisie stressed the idea of freedom e.g. freedom from formal constraints such as working for one's feudal lord, since what was required was freedom for individuals to work in factories in return for a day's wage.)

We can apply Marx's analysis to the decline of Catholicism and the rise of Protestantism. The conflict between the rising bourgeoisie and the feudal aristocracy was reflected in the area of religious belief. Hence the Catholicism which was dominant in the feudal world emphasised accepting one's position and trying to be happy with it, hence it supported the class interests of the aristocracy. However, the more individualistic Protestantism, with its stress on the freedom of men to worship in their own fashion and on the individual having his own personal relationship with God, fitted in with the individualistic ideology of the rising bourgeoisie. In this way, as new powerful groups emerge, so ideas, including religion, come to reflect their interests.

One of the cornerstones of Marx's writings is that all societies are class societies and are characterised by exploitation and potential conflict. In the same way that the feudal aristocracy and land owners exploited serfs and used them to their own benefit, so too in capitalist societies the owners of the means of production exploit wage labourers. What is required is a means of disguising this exploitation; a set of justifications and beliefs which will mask, hide and legitimate this exploitative relationship. Religion is important in this process since it suggests that the world is God given and not produced by man.

One of the consequences of this is that people are led away from any action which might change the existing structure and nature of society. Instead, there is an emphasis on accepting one's lot and doing God's will. For many Marxists the emphasis on waiting for a reward in heaven is dismissed as false consciousness which leads to political passivism.

In this way, religion is an instrument of oppression and exploitation. Religious beliefs effectively confuse and blind the mass of society into thinking that the social world is God given and hence unchangeable (see Reading 19). However, it also serves to ease the pain of oppression by promising a paradise of eternal bliss after death and so makes this life more bearable. People who suffer find their suffering eased by the thought that a channels of protest, the connection between religion and different socio-economic groups, and the connection between religious organisations and the State.

The future

In relation to the debates and problems already outlined, we ought to turn to attempts to predict the future of religion. While those who have adopted a narrow view of religion tend to see it in decline, others have tended to see it undergoing transformation. For many of the earlier writers religion served to offer an explanation of the inexplicable – it offered reassurance and a way of coming to terms with man's precarious existence. Many of these early writers also had a view of religion as a stage in man's development, thus as science increasingly narrowed the realm of the inexplicable, so religion would no longer be required. Whether science has replaced religion however, is a complex question.

Other sociologists, particularly those who had some agreement with Durkheim's analysis, began to explore the hidden or 'latent' functions of religion. While the explicit or manifest function of religion might be to provide an avenue for salvation, religion performed other unintended functions. Religion served to integrate society together, produced shared values, justified the social order, produced opportunities for emotional expression, and gave an identity to individuals and groups. Some of those who argued that these functions were necessary and indispensable argued that anything which met these functions was, by definition, religious. Hence the idea of a civil religion which although not explicitly concerned with religion as it is commonly understood, nevertheless performed the functions of religion and could therefore be regarded as religious. If we accept these assumptions then religion, in whatever guise, will always be with us.

Sociologist such as Bryan Wilson, who also owes much to the Durkheimian tradition, have argued that many of the functions of religion have been either taken over by other agencies or else, as religion has declined, not been performed. As we have suggested, he tends to view a world in which religion increasingly loses its influence and functions, with the consequences that

society becomes increasingly unstable and open to social disorder.

For Marx religion is a stage in the historical development of
society, and is bound to be replaced. He suggests that religious
thinking and practice will be gradually reduced. The implication
is that in a society of the future, where man is truly conscious of
his own ability, and aware of his true nature, there will be no
need for religious beliefs.

Once again though we should be aware of the importance of
definitions when predicting the future.

Berger and Luckmann seem to suggest that religion is a
process of constructing meaning systems by which men see,
interpret, communicate, understand and give meaning to their
lives. Because every society constructs its own world, its own
meaning system, every society is necessarily religious. That the
meaning system is Marxism, or Christianity is not important,
they may be regarded as religious in that they provide all–
embracing frameworks for human action and understanding.

Clearly many of the issues we have begun to explore rest on
problems of definition. It is this issue which shall be explored in
more detail in the following chapter.

Sociologists and religion

Many sociologists have approached religion as some kind of
collective delusion, a false diagnosis which sociology and a
scientific approach can not only explain, but explain away.
Religion is seen as a device to reinforce the collective identity, a
tool of class exploitation, an attempt to escape from the world,
an illusion to ease pain, an attempt to come to terms with the
inexplicable. What religion is not seen as, for the most part, is
true.

There are those who regard religion as a form of ideology
which serves to hide the true nature of, and reasons for,
inequality. Such an approach tends to see religion as something
which the growth of science and rationality will gradually
remove.

A second group have argued that we should study religion
from the standpoint of the religious person because we can only
understand religion if we come to see it through the eyes of

those actively involved. This approach often assumes that we can discuss, analyse and explain religious phenomena from the point of view of the actors involved, and without questioning the truth of their beliefs.

A third approach assumes that religion has a degree of truth, but that sociology can still aid our understanding of the consequences of religious belief. In this way, although worship may bring an individual closer to God, it may also integrate members of society together or ease the problems of worldly life.

These approaches suggest three standpoints concerning religious belief: the first, that the religious person is falsely conscious and unaware of the true nature of the social world as a human construct; the second, that it does not matter whether religious beliefs are true or false since what is important is the way they affect human behaviour; and the third, that there is no conflict between religion and sociology since both can help us to understand and give meaning to the world.

Much has been written in recent years over whether a sociologist can and should be 'value free', and the extent to which values affect research. While not wanting to delve into the debate it is necessary to be aware of the different approaches that have been adopted and the possible implications these might have. For these reasons it seems appropriate to declare my position as a sociologist who has religious beliefs.

better world awaits them. Indeed, in some religions, the more you suffer on earth, the more likely you are to be assured of a place in heaven, or a more favourable position in the next life. It is in this way that religion is the 'opium of the people'; it dulls the pain of oppression:

> (Religion is the sigh of the oppressed creature, the sentiment of a heartless world just as it is the spirit of a spiritless situation. It is the opium of the people.)
>
> Marx, K., *Early Writings*, Watts, London, 1962.

By promising salvation after death, by making a virtue out of suffering and by offering hope of a supernatural intervention, religion eases the pain of the exploited.

While Marx's writings offer some explanations as to why the exploited are religious there appears some ambiguity over why those who are dominant also seem to be religious. One answer is to argue that this group is not truly religious, but gives the impression it is in order to maintain the faith and the support of other groups. On the other hand Marx appears to suggest that the dominant group, in order to justify their position to themselves, come to accept that their position is due to some divine intervention. In effect both rulers and ruled are alienated and unaware of their true nature.

Like Marx, Weber argued that religion often served to justify and legitimate the existing social and economic arrangement of society. Thus for example the Hindu notion of Kharma, in which the soul passes through a series of lives, compensates for injustices in any one life. It serves to justify people's position in the social hierarchy and offers hope for the unfortunate in the next life.

Similarly Durkheim's views on religion with its effects of reaffirming the collective identity and shared values, meant that it was not generally a force connected with social change – it tended to support the existing social system.

Support for the idea of religion inhibiting social change has come from a wide variety of sources. We have already pointed to the Indian caste system and the beliefs of the sixteenth and seventeenth centuries. Another interesting analysis which has been used as evidence of religion as change inhibiting is the Halevy thesis in which Elie Halevy suggested that religion played an important role in preventing a revolution in the eighteenth and nineteenth centuries in Britain.

The period of Methodist revival in the early and mid eighteenth century was characterised by a number of economic and political problems. Halevy argues that far from leading to revolution, discontented workers came under the influence of Wesley and his colleagues, who started as Anglican clergy and were closely connected to the established order. However, he is not suggesting that the Methodist movement was consciously formed by members of the dominant group to suppress the working class and mobilise it in an anti-revolutionary direction. Rather he points to the desire of Wesley and others to breathe new life into the established church. The effect of their 'eccentric style of preaching' and 'doctrinal extravagance' however, was that they became banned from many churches and became viewed as a dissenting movement. The religious message of Wesley and his charismatic appeal; the emotional excitement and involvement of the preaching; the sense of identity and community the movement gave, and the notion of Methodism as being anti-establishment, coupled with the limited alternative avenues through which to express their discontent, served to distract significant numbers of the working class from their grievances and any impulse to rebel. The consequence of this was that Britain, unlike many other European countries at that time, was relatively free from revolutionary upheavals and sudden change.

Although this thesis has obtained some support from E. P. Thomson, we should note that it has also been criticised. According to Hobsbawm, revolutions require more than discontent and political activity – they require a socio-economic crisis, and Halevy has greatly exaggerated the religious variable and neglected others. In summarising Hobsbawm's argument Hill notes that:

> Methodism was never as potent as has been suggested, and there was no revolution because the ruling class knew when to make concessions and thus never lost control.
>
> Hill, 1973.

The accuracy of the thesis is clearly one of historical debate, but it does serve to show that religion can be an important factor in inhibiting change, even if, as Hobsbawm points out, we need to take into account other variables.

Religion as change promoting

One of Weber's central themes was that ideas and beliefs can have important consequences for the way men think and act, and only by understanding the meaning given to situations can we understand social action. He used these ideas when analysing one of his major concerns: the development of capitalism and especially what he defined as rational capitalism. For him, rational capitalism requires both normative conditions and the material conditions. In other words, the necessary values and economic conditions must be present. Only when these two are present will the transformation take place to bring about capitalism as we know it. It was this belief which led to his detailed comparative research into religious beliefs and practices.

Among the Hindus of India the belief in the caste system, in which the occupational structure offered no opportunity for mobility and where even not fulfilling your duty as determined by your caste position, could result in a less favourable reincarnation, effectively prevented economic development as found in the West. Despite the presence of developed manufacturing, considerable trade, craft guilds and appropriate monetary systems, the beliefs and practices of Hinduism effectively made the development of rational capitalism unlikely. The material structure was present, but the rational 'spirit' of capitalism was not.

Amongst Calvinists, however, magic and rituals were relatively absent and thus did not stifle a 'rational' economic view. In this sense, Calvinism did not cause the development of a capitalist ethic, but unlike other religions it did not provide an effective barrier to its development.

However, Weber did argue that not only does Calvinism not hinder the development of a rational outlook so necessary for capitalist development, but it actively produces one. Central to this line of argument is the doctrine of predestination. This is the belief that before birth a person's ultimate destiny – whether salvation or damnation – is determined. How a person acts will make no difference; an individual's fate is decided and irreversible. The problem of course is why such a belief did not lead to resignation and an acceptance of one's lot. Why did this belief lead to the spirit of capitalism where the desire to accumulate more and more money was coupled with the avoidance of using the wealth for personal enjoyment; where material acquisition and man's devotion to it became not a means to an end, but an end in itself?

The answer lies in the problem of the believer not knowing whether he was one of the saved. The solution to this dilemma was twofold. Firstly, by assuming that the individual was one of the chosen, since any doubts reflected a lack of grace. Secondly, by 'intense worldly activity', since success and the performance of good works was a sign of election, of being one of God's chosen. These were not a means of achieving salvation, but of eliminating doubts. Factors such as hard work, thrift, modesty and the avoidance of idleness, time wasting and self indulgence became signs of God's grace and an indication that the individual was one of the chosen.

Calvinist teaching then, and especially the belief in predestination, provided a strong incentive for a disciplined and very active life in the world. By practising 'inner worldly ascetism' in which they worked hard and diligently and yet were relatively austere, rather than detaching themselves from the world to pursue religious concerns, they provided a marked contrast to followers of some other religions. Furthermore, unlike other religious beliefs, such as Hinduism, where the traditional methods of producing were more important than efficient ones, with Calvinism what was important was success, as a sign of being one of the elect.

This religious view of the world and the consequences of it is what Weber means by the 'Protestant ethic'. He compares this with the 'spirit of capitalism' in which accumulating wealth and a rational attempt to maximise output are important components. For Weber the 'restless, conscientious, systematic work in a worldly calling must have been the most powerful conceivable lever for the expansion of the spirit of capitalism.' (Weber, 1974, originally published 1904–05). Thus the religious beliefs of Calvinists, coupled with the presence of the necessary economic conditions resulted in the development of a capitalist system.

One of the difficulties with Weber's work is that there appear to be two arguments in his thesis concerning the development of capitalism. On the one hand he seems to argue that Calvinism was a 'causal' factor in the development of a capitalist spirit – it was a very active force in promoting social change. On the other hand, there is the idea that Calvinism and the spirit of capitalism were very close – the ideas were in close harmony. There existed what Weber called an 'elective affinity'; not a causal relationship but an association between them. In this way, his writings on other world religions, such as Hinduism and Buddhism, aimed to show that while they impeded the development of a rational economic outlook, Calvinism did not. This is clearly different from saying that Calvinism caused capitalism.

What is clear from his analysis, however, is that if we want to understand social change, we need to take account of the effect of beliefs and ideas. He was not saying that religion always caused change, but wanted to show, through an analysis of the rise of capitalism, that it could be an important factor. Thus at the end of his most famous work on this subject he stressed that he did not want to give a one-sided causal interpretation of social change:

> But it is, of course, not my aim to substitute for a one-sided materialism an equally one-sided spiritualist causal interpretation of culture and of history. Each is equally possible, but each, if it does not serve as the preparation, but as the conclusion of an investigation, accomplishes equally little in the interest of historical truth.
>
> Weber, 1974.

Despite considerable criticism (see Readings 14, 15 and 16), Weber's work remains one of immense interest giving as it does an insight into the relationship between religion and social change. However, this is far from the only source linking change and religion. Thus, for example, some contemporary Marxists have suggested that religious imagery and symbols are important. Because religion shows the possibility of a better world, it has the potential to raise man's consciousness. Although religion may suggest that a better world is possible in a divine afterlife, this very fact may result in an awareness that the present life is far from perfect and hence in turn lead to a desire to change it.

Indeed, the work of Marx's colleague Engels suggested that some religious movements could pave the way for social change. Engels' work focused on what have become known as millenarian movements, which are often followed by those at the bottom of society. Such movements have often been seen as prepolitical i.e. the ideas and beliefs developed have later been taken up by political groups. Worsley has offered us some insight into this by suggesting that various religious groups in Melanesia can be understood as reactions to colonialism and exploitation which served to unite people together in a common bond. Such awareness and sense of shared injustice might later become transformed into political protest in which a degree of social change results.

While Marx's writings have often been interpreted as saying that religion is determined by economic factors, Marx and his followers are aware that the relationship between the two is somewhat more complex than this suggests (see Reading 20). Many contemporary Marxists have pointed out that although religious institutions such as churches may reflect the interests of the dominant groups in society, they may develop a degree of autonomy. They may develop a degree of freedom and hence not always act in the direct interests of the dominant group in society.

So far in this chapter we have seen how religion can be an agent of change or an agent of stability. We have also explored the arguments of both Marx and Weber and suggested that although their writings may have stressed one aspect or the other, they were both aware of the complex relationship between religion and social change. What we need to look at next are the factors which might result in religion being change inducing or change inhibiting.

Factors affecting the relationship between religion and social change

Charismatic leaders

Weber pointed to the power of charisma for social change, arguing that it was the 'specifically creative revolutionary force of history', (Weber, M., *Economy and Society*, Bedminster Press, New York, 1968). For Weber, charisma was a type of authority vested in an individual due to his or her perceived qualities and powers, which were not usually seen in others.

Such authority is often seen as outside the accepted institutional framework, and as such is viewed as new and challenging. Wesley might provide an example. Charismatic leaders are often religious, primarily because religion can form a basis of authority – thus someone who can claim their authority from God may have considerable impact.

Studies of social change have often revealed an effective leader who not only condemns the existing social arrangements, but by his charismatic nature is able to motivate and direct others towards a new goal. We do not have to look far to see the influence of such figures in recent years. Ayatollah Khomeini and the overthrow of the Shah in Iran provides a good example. However, there is a danger that we produce a 'great man' image of social change, and clearly a wide variety of other factors must be taken into account. What is suggested is that charismatic leaders, who are often religious leaders, may provide a focus for discontent and a view of a better world, which in turn may act as a catalyst for social change.

One problem is that while some of these leaders may reaffirm the existing order (perhaps unintentionally as has been suggested in the case of Wesley), others may reject it. What is significant, however, is that charismatic leaders are often religious leaders who emerge unexpectedly, and have revolutionary consequences. Whether they lead to change depends, amongst other things, upon their message, and perhaps also their social background.

Beliefs and practices

We have already noted Weber's idea that while the religious beliefs and practices of Calvinists led to social change, other religious beliefs meant that change was unlikely. In part this reflects his distinction between an 'other worldly' outlook and a 'this worldly' outlook. The inner worldly asceticism of the Calvinist tradition encouraged activity in the world, not inactivity and a retreat from the world. If a particular system of beliefs proclaims that mankind is powerless to change the world because it is given and controlled by God, then change is less likely, at least intentionally. Similarly, those religions which stress that the social order is a consequence of a person's actions in the past are unlikely to lead to change, since such beliefs effectively justify and legitimate existing social arrangements.

Some religious movements, however, are not only active in the world, but seek to change it. One example could be the followered of Sun Myung Moon – the Unification Church, or 'Moonies' as they are frequently known. They are a movement who believe in the 'Second Coming' when God will set up a new order on earth. Their movement is intended to begin the process of establishing the 'Kingdom of God on earth' in preparation for the 'Lord of the Second Advent'. They are attempting to bring about social change, and although some have argued that the eventual death of their leader will lead to the group dying with him, others are not so sure. The group has already developed a well organised bureaucratic structure, their own family structure and educational institutions. Whether such a group will bring about widespread social changes is doubtful, but the important point to note in the context of our present discussion is that their religious beliefs and practices are working towards it.

A similar analysis could be made of the Black Muslim Movement which began in 1930 with the arrival of Elijah Muhammad who preached about the true heritage of blacks and their true religion, Islam. The movement was anti-white and attracted considerable support in later years, including Malcolm X (the 'X' signifies an ex-member of white society), and Cassius Clay, who took the Muslim named Muhammad Ali. Their belief in this own divinity and their aim of establishing the rightful position of blacks in American society may well have had some success in bringing about limited social change in terms of legal rights.

Relationship to society

In a society where religion is seen as a distinct and separate institution, it is less likely to be closely integrated with other spheres of society and may be more likely to become an independent factor in social change. It is difficult to see the Church of England with its formal and informal connections with the State as a body which will present much challenge to the present system.

Those groups, such as sects, which tend to be in opposition to the wider society and have few ties with it, may be more likely to lead to social change. They are frequently regarded as being on the fringes of society and not only oppose it, but have little to be lost if society undergoes change. On the other hand, where religion permeates throughout society and is closely integrated with other areas, then religion may be an important element in inhibiting change.

The social status of religious membership

Religious organisations may be closely connected to the stratification system. Although not true of all sectarian movements and all churches, there appears to be a tendency for established churches to have congregations which are disproportionally drawn from the upper status groups, and for sectarian movements to attract less privileged groups. If this is the case, it seems unlikely that religious protest will arise from the churches, since the established social arrangements serve their members' in terests. However, while movements such as the Black Muslims do recruit from the lower social strata, recent research suggests that other sects, such as the Moonies and other new religious movements, do not.

While we shall be exploring these issues in more depth when we look at sects, it is possible to make some generalisations relating membership of religious organisations to social change. Where established churches are seen as being linked to the dominant groups in society, and where there is dissatisfaction with the existing distribution of society's rewards, sects may be seen by deprived members of society as a vehicle to air their grievances and effect social change.

The presence of alternative avenues to change

One of the explanations for the growth of new religious movements during the 1960s and 1970s, particularly in the United States, was the absence of any other avenues for social change. Writers such as Wallis argue that increased disenchantment and and discontent with the way society was operating led to attempts to transform it. One of these was by political protest, demonstrations, etc., but when these proved ineffective, some new religious movements were seen as another avenue – if change could not be achieved using secular methods perhaps a religious alternative might achieve results. While these groups do not appear to have transformed the American way of life, it is important to note that the inadequacy of other avenues for change led to a growth in seeing religious movements as possible soures.

A similar argument might be made in the case of religious protest movements such as those in Melanesia which have often been seen as consequences of colonialism and exploitation. The absence of alternative avenues for change meant that religious protest movements developed. Worsley suggests that where political organisations were present, the response to such exploitation tended towards religious escapism rather than towards potential revolutionary religious movements (Worsley, P. M., *The Trumpet Shall Sound*, MacGibbon and Kee, London, 1957).

E. P. Thompson's views on the role of Methodism in Britain during the period 1790–1830 might also be referred to. He argues that prior to this time the working classes had considerable hope for political change, and they turned to religion only when these hopes were thwarted:

> Whenever hope revived, religious revivalism was set aside, only to reappear with renewed fervour upon the ruins of the political messianism which had been overthrown.
>
> Thompson E. P., *The Making of the English Working Class*,
>   Penguin, Middlesex, 1968.

Organisational structure

A religion with a centralised priesthood, hierarchy of paid officials and bureaucratic structure, has considerable influence on the group's direction and purpose. Such organisational structures are often associated with established churches, which, as we have suggested, due to their integration with society are less likely to be agents of change. The centrality of priests often shown in formal worship makes them an important potential influence on the direction the movement takes.

Sects, which many have pointed to as the religious groups most likely to lead to change, tend to develop into denominations or movements which have evolved a hierarchy of officials and an increasing acceptance of the norms and values of society. Such a process may mean that religious groups which oppose society are increasingly likely to become integrated with it.

On the other hand, religious groups which have large organisational support outside the immediate situation may be in a better position to criticise existing social and political arrangements. Hence the role of Roman Catholic priests in Latin America and their outspoken condemnation of some political systems. Thus some Roman Catholic priests condemned the

Somoza regime in Nicaragua and aided the overthrow by the Sandinistas. A movement without such a large external organisational structure may have been more susceptible to repression. At the same time, however, the larger organisation may attempt to control its clergy and suppress any initiatives for change. For example Bruce Kent's involvement with CND (Campaign for Nuclear Disarmament) led to some criticism, and four Catholic priests holding government positions in Nicaragua were recently asked to resign or face being defrocked.

Conclusion

The debate concerning the relationship between religion and social change is clearly complex. The early writers, notably Marx and Weber, although emphasising different sides to the argument, did imply that religion could be both change inhibiting and change promoting. Recent research has attempted to explain some of the factors which might determine the direction of the influence of religious organisations, although clearly more work needs to be done.

What has been suggested is that where there is an absence of a charismatic leader opposing the present social arrangements, where religious beliefs stress that man is powerless to change the world, where there is a complex organisational structure which is tied to the established order, where membership is drawn from upper status groups and where alternative avenues are available, religion is less likely to be an agent of social change.

5 Religious sects

Although sects vary considerably, a number of general characteristics can be outlined, although each sect will manifest these characteristics in differing degrees. Furthermore, sects are not static – they undergo change, and so over a period of time some attributes may become more or less important, or absent altogether.

1 Voluntary. Sects are voluntary organisations, although for children born into sects which have isolated themselves from wider society the opportunities to experience anything else are somewhat limited.

2 Charismatic authority. The sociological concept of charisma comes from Weber. He defined charisma as:

> a certain quality of an individual personality, by virtue of which he is considered as extraordinary and treated as endowed with supernatural, superhuman, or at least exceptional powers or qualities.
>
> Weber, 1968.

Thus the leader of the Hare Krishna movement is seen as 'His Divine Grace', and the followers of Bhagwan Shree Rajneesh see their leaders as the only living 'Enlightened Master'. However, we should note that charismatic authority tends to be transient, since when the leader dies, his charisma tends to die with him.

3 Group superiority. Sect members tend to believe that they are a select and elite group. They are the ones who are 'saved', 'enlightened', or have experienced the 'truth'. The concept of an 'elect' or chosen people is well known in Christianity, but is also prevalent in non-Christian sects.

4 Strict discipline. Sect members are expected to devote themselves to the sect, and they may have little time left from the activities demanded of members. In all sects, members are expected to conform to certain rules concerning conduct. There

tends to be an emphasis on 'devotions' and 'missionary' activity e.g. amongst the Mormons a two year period of missionary activity is compulsory for men.

5 Repression of individuality. In many sects, such as the Moonies, individuality is stifled and attempts may be made to cut themselves off from the past. In some sects, for instance Hare Krishna, new members may take on a new name, and contact with family and previous friends be very restricted. Personal responsibility may be surrendered and little opportunity given for freedom of thought.

Sect development

Many classical sociologists of religion tended to see a very close relationship between church and sect. The tendency of churches to compromise their stance and become integrated into the wider society would lead to some members feeling that the Church was no longer faithful to its traditional views and beliefs. Some members would break away and form sect–like groups which would reject the values of wider society, deny the need for an established hierarchy within the group and demand intense commitment and loyalty from its members.

In time it was felt that these sects would themselves begin to adopt church-like qualities. Once this happened, the sect also became vulnerable to breakaway movements, and the process repeated itself. Therefore the connection between churches and sects was seen as a continual circulation between the two types of religious groups.

However, while this processs may have occurred historically, sects today do not generally arise out of conflict with established churches or out of protest against them. Generally, sects appear to be created by those who are outside the Church and there appears little relationship between these two types of organisation or the people who belong to them.

Classical sociologists also pointed out that religious belief was closely related to the social stratification. Different groups in society have varying interests and life chances and respond differently to different religions. Thus, for example, Weber argues that the nature of bureaucratic work in terms of routine and order would result in 'an absolute lack of feeling of a need for salvation' (Weber, 1968) amongst this group. Different social strata will interpret religion and its message in the light of their own circumstances and experiences.

To which social groups then will sects appeal? Weber suggests that such groups are likely to emerge amongst the underprivileged; those who are towards the bottom of the social hierarchy. Such groups develop a 'Theodicy of Disprivilege' – a religious explanation for why they are in their position. However, such an explanation does more than this, it makes them one of the 'elite', since sect membership often promises a privileged afterlife which will be denied to those who are not members. The exclusiveness of many sects with their distinctive styles of worship, strict patterns of behaviour and rejection of wider society, means that members identify with their sects and consider themselves superior to those who are above them in the stratification system. They may not have the economic and social standing of others in society, but sect members have the promise of salvation and the knowledge that they are 'enlightened'.

However, it appears that sects do not only attract the disadvantaged, which might appear to falsify Weber's argument. One way in which we can account for why membership of sects is not confined to the disadvantaged is by the concept of 'relative deprivation'. This concept points to the need to look at subjective assessments of how a person perceives his or her position in society. Thus, members of the middle classes who may be relatively better off than others, may see themselves as disadvantaged, or at least perceive a gap between how much they have and how much they consider they should have. For such middle-class groups, sect membership may serve to demonstrate to themselves and others their uniqueness and difference from those around them.

This notion of relative deprivation is usually discussed in economic terms, but as Glock and Stark point out, there are other forms of deprivation, each of which may have important implications for the type of religious movements which develop. For them, deprivation refers to:

> any and all of the ways that an individual or group may be, or feel disadvantaged in comparison either to other individuals or

groups or to an internalised set of standards.

Glock, C. and Stark R., Religion and Society in Tension,
Rand McNally, Chicago, 1965.

Such deprivation may be economic, social, organismic, ethical or psychic, although an individual or group may experience a number of these.

Economic deprivation refers to the unequal distribution of income and access to resources. Social deprivation refers to the distribution of prestige, power and status. Organismic depriva tion includes the ways in which people are disadvantaged through physical factors, such as blindness and general ill health. Ethical deprivation concerns the possible conflicts between the ideals of society and those of individuals or groups, e.g. where a craftsman's concern for excellence may conflict with the demands of mass production. Finally, what the authors call psychic deprivation, occurs when people find themselves without a meaningful value system with which to interpret and organise the world. This may occur as the result of social deprivations whereby people are denied access to rewards and thus lose commitment to existing values.

Glock and Stark argue that a necessary condition for the development of any sect is a feeling of deprivation. However, a number of other factors are also required: the deprivation must be shared, no existing arrangements for the resolution of such deprivation are perceived, and finally, a leadership must emerge.

Such a schema may help us to understand the widespread growth of sects in America in the 1960s, especially amongst ethnic minorities. Suffering economic and social deprivation, and denied any realistic hope of significant change through the political system, they turned towards religious sects such as the Black Muslim movement which promised to ease their situation.

Coupled with the idea of relative deprivation, is the argument that sects frequently appear to develop in conditions of social change and disruptive social processes. These two factors may well be linked since social change, in which traditional norms, values and way of life are challenged, may result in a feeling of relative deprivation. This may be particularly true if we use Glock and Stark's term of relative deprivation and include ethical and psychic deprivation. As Wilson notes:

The sense of cultural retardation among rural people, the

sense of lost community among newly arrived urban immig-
rants, the feelings of inadequacy among native populations
impressed by the evidence of more advanced technology, and
the awareness of life-styles and opportunities available only to
others – are all conditions that may be conducive to new
'world changing' responses.

Wilson, 1970.

It is this way that Wilson attempts to explain the rise of
Methodism in England, which he argues is a response by a
particular group, the new urban working class, to the disruption
and uncertainty of life in the new industrial areas. Similarly, the
so-called 'cargo cults' of Melanesia who believe that the 'cargo' –
the wealth of the Europeans – can be obtained for themselves,
may be seen as a response to rapid social change and the feeling
of relative deprivation. In a situation of change and uncertainty,
sects offer the warmth and support of a strong community, they
provide meanings and explanations, they offer a distinct life style
with rules and procedures, they allow identification with a wider
purpose and a reason for living (see Reading 22).

While this explanation of sect development in terms of relative
deprivation and social change appears plausible we should be
aware of the problems which surround it. For example, why is it
that some who experience such processes don't join sects, or else
resolve the problems in different ways? Furthermore, little
research has been done on the different types of sectarian
responses which have developed. While some have argued that
tradition, the accessibility of political channels, and demographic factors (inhabitants from small towns and rural communities may be more accustomed to defining the world in religious
terms) may be important variables, it still remains unclear why
the religious response is chosen.

Studies of recent sectarian responses, particularly those which
developed in the 1960s and 1970s, have offered a number of new
and interesting insights. In particular, and unlike many other
similar movements in the past, they appeared to be particularly
attractive to the young, and also to the relatively affluent. The
simple and ascetic life style of many people attracted to these
movements was a marked contrast to their social origins. A
number of attempts have been made to explain the development
of such movements and their membership.

Some have linked the growth of Krishna Consciousness, Moonies and the Happy-Healthy-Holy Organisation (3HO), etc., to various changes in society, and especially the idea of secularisation. For writers such as Bryan Wilson, the very factors which cause churches to lose support and influence, encourages the emergence of sects as a rejection of the increased secular nature of society.

For Wilson, the growth of religious sects can be linked to the movement from what Töennies called 'Gemeinschaft' to 'Gesellschaft' forms of society. The usual translation of these terms is into 'community' and 'association'.

The 'Gemeinschaft' society is characterised by an emphasis on community with social cohesion, commitment and a sharing of common attitudes, values and aims. The 'Gesellschaft' society is one in which the social bonds uniting people are voluntary, and self-interest dominates. Here the picture is of a large-scale impersonal society in which people may associate, but this is far removed from the sense of community and integration found in 'Gemeinschaft'. The inevitable transition from one to the other, according to Wilson, leads to a decline in religion, except in sects which provide a haven of 'Gemeinschaft' in the impersonal and modern world.

Sects, he argues, attract because of the:

attention extended to potential members; the care and concern that is manifested; the warmth and support of a strong community; the provision of meanings; the opportunity for expresssion; identification with a purpose wider than one's previous social involvements; the availability of answers to specific questions and activities which become a raison d'etre for living. Subsequently, the individual finds opportunities for status, for self-respect and for the occasions on which to command esteem; he becomes settled to a definitite life-style which stands in sharp contrast with the normlessness and shapelessness of life in the wider society.

Wilson, 1982.

Wilson's idea can also be linked to Bellah's explanation of the growth of sects from the 1960s onwards in terms of a 'crisis of meaning (Bellah, 1976). For Bellah, American culture had traditionally been based on 'utilitarian individualism' – the idea that the individual should strive for himself, use his talents in a society which is open and aspire to the goals of economic consumption and achievement. In the 1960s, such ideas began to be questioned. There was increasing doubt as to whether the Utopia of the American Dream was really utopian. Was society instead suffering an increased loss of humanity? Such questions, coupled with events such as the Vietnam War, the Black Civil Rights campaigns and the growth of alternative meanings systems, led to a rejection by some sections of society of 'utilitarian individualism'. In particular, it was the young who adopted these new religions with their emphasis on inner experience, harmony and close relationships with others. Such movements, especially those which derived from the East, were seen as being uncontaminated by the dominant parent culture and, as such, were viewed as an alternative – as a 'counter culture'.

Sects and denominations

Denominations are usually regarded as an intermediate type of religious organisation between church and sect. They are less at odds with society at large, are tolerant of and tolerated by other religious groups and generally have a more formalised form of worship with a hierarchy of paid officials. H. R. Niebuhr's study of religion in the USA led him to believe that sects were necessarily transient of short lived, and tended to develop into denominations or else wither away (Niebuhr, H. R., *The Social Sources of Denominationalism*, Holt, New York, 1929).

Like others, Niebuhr argued that sects were closely linked to social circumstances and to some extent religious beliefs and practices are conditioned by these. In the beginning, sect members are all volunteers and have a high degree of commitment which is often shown in the form of respect and deference to a charismatic leader. However, as time goes on, a number of factors result in changes in the structure of the sect and the commitment and activities of the group:

1 New members by birth generally do not have the same commitment as original members. Furthermore, with the arrival of a second generation, the group becomes more concerned with socialisation and education. This brings it increasingly into contact with the outside world.

2 The death of a charismatic leader may also serve to threaten

the group, since successors rarely have the authority of their predecessor. Weber also noted the tendency for charismatic leadership to necessarily undergo various changes – the 'routinisation' of charisma. This form of organisation, because of its success, must cope with the day-to-day concerns of the group. There is a tendency for bureauractic structures to develop and, with this, charismatic authority tends to recede.

3 Over time, sect members often undergo a process of social mobility. The sect preaches hard work, thrift, ascetism and deferred rewards. Such activity ultimately brings them wealth and a measure of security. As Niebuhr argues, the 'most impor tant among the causes of the decline . . . to denominations is the influence of economic success.' (Niebuhr, 1929). Such success means that they become less hostile to the world and gradually reintegrated into it.

Through the use of a number of examples such as the growth of Methodism and its eventual development into a denomination, Niebuhr makes a generalisation concerning the movement from sects to denominations. However, research suggests that not all sects follow this development, and only those with certain features are likely to become denominationalised.

This increasing awareness of the difficulty of generalising about sects has led to attempts to categorise them. Wilson bases his categorisation on how sects respond to the issue which concerns all religious groups: 'What shall we do to be saved?' (Wilson, 1970). He argues that there are seven different ways in which sects have responded to this question which produces his seven-fold classification: conversionist, revolutionist, introversionist, manipulationist, thaumaturgical, reformist and utopian.

For Wilson, the sects which have become denominationalised have tended to be the conversionist sects – those sects which argue that the only to salvation is by being 'born again'. Such sects attempt to save souls and convert others, often by widespread evangelism. This need for widespread evangelism and structures to assist and help the converted leads to bureaucratic structures, the development of an established clergy, etc. However, Wilson also argues that the internal organisation of sects is affected by outside factors. For example, conversionist sects have tended to work largely among urbanising and industrialising populations – those that may be suffering from the effects of social change. Such groups are likely to be marginal in society only temporarily, and thus their initial reason for a sectarian response is unlikely to persist. Following Niebuhr's theory, these groups are likely to become denominations. Such a process can be seem amongst Baptists and Pentecostalists.

Other forms of sects, however, do not show the process of denominationalisation. Introversionist sects attempt to withdraw from the world; their community becomes the only place of salvation. The world is seen as evil, and the way to salvation lies in withdrawing from it. There is little interest in evangelism since inner illumination is difficult to convey and there is the danger of being contaminated by outsiders. Such sects, argues Wilson, have generally been small and have tended to preserve their sectarian nature and beliefs by insulating themselves from the wider society.

While most research and debate has focused on the movement from sects to denominations, we should remember that the other direction is also possible, i.e. denominations may develop into a sect, or at least sectarian movements may break away. The history of the Salvation Army, for example, shows a movement from denomination to sect. Similarly, James Jones' People's Temple which hit the headlines in December 1978 after 900 members committed suicide in Guyana, began as part of the accepted American Christian Church (Disciples of Christ).

The future

Studies of sects tend to show that many have a relatively short life, although new sects are continually coming into existence as the old die. This reflects the fact that societies and sects, are not static but are undergoing change. If, as a number of writers have suggested, religious belief and practice is conditioned by social factors, then societal change will result in changes in the religious dimension. This does not mean that religion is necessarily determined by economic or political factors, but that in trying to understand religious organisations such as sects, we must take into account such factors.

Furthermore, we should be aware that sect membership is relatively small. Although statistics are difficult to obtain and even more difficult to interpret, (which groups, for example, do we define as churches, which as denominations and which as sects?), they do suggest that sect membership is small, certainly in this country, when compared to membership of established churches and denominations. A number of factors which we have analysed clearly suggest that sects may be transitory. We have previously noted Niebuhr's thesis concerning the trend from sect to denomination, and while Wilson argues that some sects are more permanent than others, he does observe that many of the contemporary sects which grew up in the 1960s and 1970s appear to be particularly attractive to the young, which may prove to be an unstable basis for their continuation. Furthermore, given the radical commitment many of the sects demand, we must question the extent to which they can retain and increase their membership, although a number of sources have pointed to the strict discipline of sect members, and the mass media has stressed aspects of 'brainwashing' by which it is believed that some sects control and ensure the loyalty of their followers.

However, we have already seen the dangers of generalising about sects, and when talking about the future of sects it is possible that some types may be more resilient than others. Roy Wallis suggests that while some sects appear to be stagnating, others appear to be growing and prospering.

One way of explaining this is to conceive of sects as being ranged on a continuum, at one end world-rejecting sects and at the other end, world-affirming. World-rejecting sects are easier to recognise, they have a clear concept of God and see man as plagued by greed and insecurity. They tend to condemn modern industrial society and call for a life of service and suppression of self-interest. Members of such groups may spend long hours distributing the movement's literature, in devotional rituals and in the general communal life style of such movements.

An example is provided by the followers of the Indian mystic Bhagwan Shree Rajneesh who have built their own town in Oregon, USA, complete with airport and a television network.

World-affirming movements, in contrast, appear to lack many of the characteristics of established religions. God is not usually referred to and, if reference is made, then he tends to be seen 'as a diffuse, amorphous and imminent force in the universe, present most particularly within oneself.' (Wallis, 1978). Such movements may see the world as having many good features, which conflicts sharply with the condemnation of society by world-rejecting movements. World-affirming movements also picture mankind as having enormous physical and mental potential. Such potential has previously only been available to a select few, but with the revelations of a guru such potential will be open to all, and without withdrawing from the world or going through the rigours of the world-rejecting movements. Not only will the follower be shown ways of achieving the social and economic benefits of society, but this will involve little sacrifice in terms of present life styles.

Transcendental meditation provides an example of world-affirming movements. According to its leader, Maharishi Mahesh Yogi, all men have a divine nature, but few have learnt to experience it. What is required is meditation for fifteen or so minutes, twice a day, by the use of a mantra (a word or phrase upon which to meditate) – on payment of a fee each individual can receive instruction in meditation and their own personal mantra. Such meditation will not only result in experiencing the 'Divine Nature', but will also lead to deep rest and relaxation, an improvement in the quality of life and the development of the full potential of mind and body.

Wallis sees both world-rejecting and world-affirming movements as products of the turmoil of the 1960s and 1970s. According to Wallis, the idealism of these times was not fulfilled and two responses were available, either rejection of the world and 'dropping out' or attempts to transform the world by protest, anti-war demonstrations, etc. Both of these responses failed. It is in this context that the world-rejecting faiths grew, since it was seen that secular atempts at changing the world had failed. Not only were such movements attractive in terms of their opposition to the world, but the idea of a caring, sharing society was obtainable through communal living. Another response to the inability to change the world was to accommodate oneself to it. The world-affirming movements did not offer the promise of a new society, they offered the techniques and skills to improve and gain the results of this world.

The prosperity of the 1960s and early 1970s has given way to the recession of the 1980s. At the same time, after tremendous growth corresponding to increased affluence, the world-rejecting movements have begun to stagnate. Not only this, but they have begun the change. Those sects which occupied the middle ground along the continuum, such as Divine Light have increasingly moved towards world-affirmation; meditation is now increasingly a consumer commodity to gain the riches of the world rather than as a way to self enlightenment. At the same time, the increasingly precarious job market means that fewer people are prepared to risk a future by withdrawing from the world, while world-affirming movements offer the possiblity of enhancing one's prospects.

While Wallis offers a picture in which sects become increasingly worldly, the charismatic leadership of many sects may lead to a crisis of leadership succession. The centrality of A. C. Bhaktivedanta, leader of Krishna Consciousness, and Yogi Bhajan of the Happy-Healthy-Holy Organisation suggests that such groups will not survive their deaths, at least in their present form. Others suggest, however, that the futures of such groups rest not on the groups themselves, but on the developments in society. Bellah (1976) describes three possible scenarios for American society: liberal, traditional authoritarian and revolutionary, and argues that each of these will affect the future of sects.

In the liberal scenario, America will continue to devote itself to the accumulation of wealth, and the utilitarian individualism will remain. Bellah sees a role for sects in such a society, since they may provide for the expression of frustration and anger at the system, but in such a way that the system itself is not threatened. The second picture is of a right-wing traditional authoritarian structure in which conservative Protestant fundamentalism would dominate. It is unlikely in a society like this that sects such as the ones previously mentioned would be allowed to operate. The third alternative, revolutionary, would bring social, cultural and structural change. This scenario pictures a society in which utilitarian individualism gives way to a great concern *with* harmony *with* nature and *between* people, coupled perhaps with a simpler material life style. While such a view seems utopian, it is under these conditions that the contemporary sects would be neither safety valve nor persecuted minority, but the forerunners of a new age.

While the future of sects is partly dependent on the nature of society, it seems likely that some form of sectarian movement will continue to be with us. Historically, sects have developed to meet the needs of different groups – the ethnic minorities, cultural and socially deprived, etc. In a world which seems likely to continue to develop feelings of dissatisfaction and alientation, so too the search for meaning and alternative life styles will continue. For some at least, these alternatives will be sought in sectarian movements.

6 Religion and science as belief systems

In this chapter we shall explore some of the ideas which have derived from the influential work of Berger and Luckmann, and particularly whether science and religion can be viewed as 'belief systems'.

According to Berger and Luckmann the sociology of religion should be concerned with all forms of belief which enable people to make sense of and interpret the world. What is required is for the sociology of religion to be combined with the sociology of knowledge in an attempt to explore and explain areas of belief which guide man's understanding and seek to explain events. The sociology of religion thus has to deal with a variety of religious and 'pseudo-religious' belief systems which have not usually been thought of as its province of inquiry, including 'scientism', 'psychologism' and 'communism'.

They argue that a 'universe of meaning' exists in every society, or perhaps more accurately a number of such universes, one of which may be dominant. These universes are ways of seeing, interpreting, remembering and communicating group and individual experiences and are given to the individual from birth. The child grows up with and is socialised into a particular way of understanding, thinking about and explaining the world. This universe is a social construct; it is socially derived, socially sustained and socially legitimated. Such a universe may be a religious one, a scientific one, a magical one, etc.

However, this does not mean that any universe of meaning or belief system is always clearly understood. Consider why some people throw salt over their shoulder if they knock over the salt cellar. Clearly their belief that this is bad luck affects their behaviour, but most people would have a hard time explaining why such an act is considered bad luck. (It is also worth mentioning that it is not unusual for people to hold beliefs which appear to conflict with each other.)

Using this notion of universes of meaning it is possible to make a number of observations. Firstly, if we accept that different belief systems exist within societies and between them, then we have to accept that there are different ways of assessing and conceptualising things such as 'truth', 'accuracy' and 'proof'. The Christian's idea of 'truth' being the word of God is somewhat different from truth as understood by scientists. These two groups will use the concept differently and it will affect the way they think, act and explain the world in which they live.

The idea of a belief system also implies the existence of a body of knowledge, although people may trust in, believe and accept a body of knowledge without fully understanding it and will also tend to accept what 'experts' say. This leads us to another point; the existence of a body of knowledge tends to lead to the development of groups or individuals who claim to understand the contents of a particular belief system and who have particular talents in the field. Examples of these experts in a particular field of knowledge include clergy, scientists and witches.

Such people may enjoy high status in the community due to their proficiency in a given field. They are likely to hold their views strongly and reject other belief systems as being inappropriate. For some Christians the evolutionary theory of man is not only wrong but it is ungodly. Scientists on the other hand might argue that a belief in Adam and Eve is naïve and does not fit the evidence available. It is interesting to note how the different belief systems use the content of the belief to dismiss alternatives for example, Christians might talk of an explanation as ungodly, while scientists might call it unscientific.

A final observation is that different interests may be at work to try and question or maintain these belief systems, and although one may be dominant there will probably by others attempting to gain increased acceptance and discredit alternatives. This can be seen to apply to the fields of both religion and science – it might be possible to interpret the church's attempt to squash evolutionary theories and 'scientific' explanations of the origin of man in this way. While the history of the church may be seen as an attempt to keep out interpretations which differ from established views, so too science attempts to reject explantatory frameworks which conflict with established ones. The medical community's traditional rejection of, and scepticism towards, acupuncture and homoeopathy provide examples.

If we accept that the sociology of religion should concern itself with all belief systems, it might be possible to study religion and science in a similar way. However, many would argue that the logic and rationality of scientific understanding is very different from religion. But is it? Some philosophers of science have argued that religious belief systems and modern scientific belief systems have a number of similarities. Firstly, they both search for explanation by looking for broad, underlying factors which can explain the apparent diversity and disorder in the world. Secondly, they may both attempt to place things in a causal relationship. Thirdly, they are both attempts to come to terms with the inexplicable. While for some this may be seen as the will of God which is beyond understanding, for others a rational, scientific explanation is available, although perhaps we have not discovered it.

A number of writers have also criticised the assumption that science is concerned with objectivity, gathering the 'facts' and interpreting them impartially. Kuhn, for example, notes how scientists carry out reseach with a particular view of the world – what he calls a paradigm – which affects the proccsses of inquiry, the type of evidence gathered and the way the evidence is viewed. This suggests that science may be a social construct, a belief system which influences the way people view and understand the world, in the same way that religion does.

The classical sociologists attempted to relate both science and religion to the wider social context. Thus for Marx, science, as well as religion, is a social construct, and the form it takes is dependent upon the powerful groups in society. Hence in outlining the Marxist approaches to science Mulkay notes:

> the direction taken by modern science, its rapid rate of growth and the manner of its application in industry and government can be seen to have been largely determined by technological objectives of a particular group . . .
>
> Mulkay, M., *Science and the Sociology of Knowledge,*
> Allen & Unwin, London, 1979.

We could also link this to the Marxist idea that the ruling ideas in any age are the ideas of the dominant group and serve their interests. While in the past such dominant ideas may have been religious and are now scientific, they both support and act in the interests of the dominant group. While more detailed work needs to be done on how scientific belief systems work in this way, what is significant for our discussion is that both science and religion can be studied as belief systems.

If we reinterpret the sociology of religion so that it becomes a part of the sociology of knowledge as Berger and Luckmann suggest, where does it lead us? Firstly, as we have seen, it leads to a broadening of the field of inquiry to include belief systems generally and therefore breaks away from an analysis of religion solely in terms of religious institutions. Secondly, the fact that different belief systems may be in operation means that they compete with one another. Berger and Luckmann argue that this 'market character' of such systems is an important characteristic deserving detailed analysis. Thirdly, it leads to a consideration of religion alongside other agencies which influence social knowledge. In this way the sociology of religion and the sociology of the mass media both explore the creation and legitimation of social knowledge and belief systems. It is for this reason that a number of recent texts have tended to cover religion and the mass media in the same chapter. Finally, it returns the sociology of religion to the very heart of sociology where it becomes a study of the way man perceives and interprets the world around him, and the subsequent ways he acts in it.

PART 3

Statistics and documentary readings

7 Statistics on religion

Many of those who argue that religion is in decline employ a wide range of statistical material to support their case. The following three figures are taken from the 1983 edition of the Church of England's *Church Statistics*, and provide examples of the sort of material often used by those who claim secularisation is taking place.

Figure 7.1   Selected membership comparisons 1960–1981 Provinces of Canterbury and York (excluding Europe)

Baptisms

Year	Live births 000s	Infant baptisms 000s	Infant baptism rates per 1000 live births	Baptisms of other persons 000s
1	2	3	4	5
1960	744	412	554	11
1962	796	423	531	12
1964	832	437	526	11
1966	808	413	511	10
1968	778	381	492	9
1970	745	347	466	8
1973	640	298	465	7
1976	553	237	428	8
1978	565	217	383★	36
1980	621	226	365★	40
1981	600	219	365★	39

*Figure 7.2   Selected membership comparisons 1960–1981, Provinces of
Canterbury and York (excluding Europe)*

Parochial Easter and Christmas Communicants

Year	Estimated mid-year population aged 15 and over 000s	Easter communicants 000s	Easter communicant rates per 1000 population aged 15 and over	Christmas communicants 000s	Christmas communicant rates per 1000 population aged 15 and over
1	2	3	4	5	6
1960	33,395	2,339	70	2,074	62
1962	34,211	2,347	69	1,893	55
1964	34,714	2,142	62	1,926	55
1966	35,078	2,075	59	2,024	58
1968	35,273	1,975	56	1,789	51
1970	35,450	1,814	51	1,689	48
1973	35,627	1,684	47	1,720	48
1976	36,060	1,681	47	1,695	47
1978	36,438	1,698	47	1,785	49
1980	36,924	1,732	47	1,807	49
1981	37,566	1,691	45	1,617	43

Figures 7.1, 7.2 and 7.3 reproduced by kind permission of the
Central Board of Finance of the Church of England from *Church
Statistics 1983* (CIO Publishing, 1983).

Like all statistics, however, these need to be treated with a
great deal of caution. For example, the baptism figures from
1978 onwards are not directly comparable with previous ones
because different definitions of what constitutes infant baptisms
have been used. Hence the decrease in these baptism figures, and
the subsequent growth in the 'other persons' category, may
simply be due to these changes in definition and classification.

Not only is it difficult to compare such statistics over time, but
it is very difficult to understand what they mean or signify. In
1980, for example, the Church of England identified 27 million

*Figure 7.3   Confirmation 1960–1982 Provinces of Canterbury and York
(excluding Europe)*

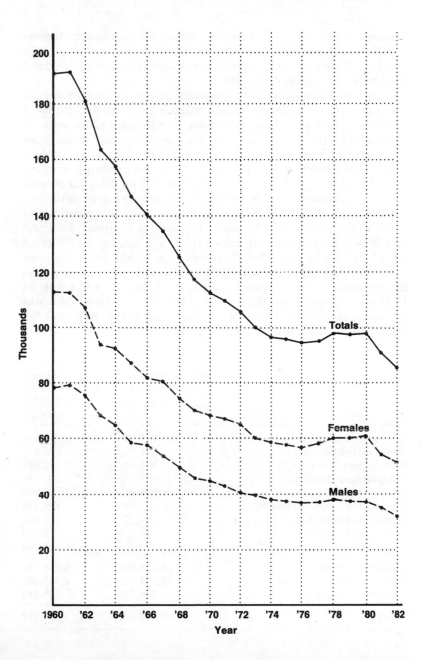

baptised, 9 million confirmed, 1.8 million on the church electoral rolls, and 1.2 million actually attending church on an average Sunday. Which of these figures represents Church of England members or 'religious' people?

In an attempt to make the situation clearer many commentators have used the categories of professing Christians, affiliated Christians, and practising Christians. Professing Christians, as defined by the *World Christian Encyclopaedia,* are those who publically identify themselves as Christians when asked their religion in various polls. Affiliated Christians are those who are regarded as being 'known to the churches'. Practising Christians are those who are active in church by gathering for worship.

But such categories also have difficulties. The following figure gives a comparison of Christian churches in England, Scotland and Wales. One column is drawn from the number of affiliated members of Christian churches drawn up by the *World Christian Encyclopaedia* and based on 1970 figures, and the other is based on the number of adult church members on the electoral rolls in 1980 and is drawn from the *UK Church Handbook.* These may also be seen as 'affiliated' in the sense that many may not be 'practising' Christians.

Figure 7.4

	W.C.E. 1970 Affiliated Adults	UK C.H. 1980 Adult Members
Anglican churches	10,155,738	2,158,888
Methodist churches	691,830	536,416
Baptist churches	303,518	251,425
Independent churches	474,349	209,756
Presbyterian churches	1,774,410	1,579,982
African/West Indian churches	52,189	106,296
Pentecostal churches	94,276	89,066
Lutheran churches	18,633	15,883
Other churches	309,703	121,163
Total Protestant	13,874,646	5,068,875
Roman Catholic churches	4,278,595	2,341,801
Orthodox churches	234,200	105,841
Total	18,387,441	7,516,517

The differences between these two figures are clearly considerable, especially for the Anglican churches. While the ten year time difference may account for some of the variation, it seems likely that a major factor is the difference in the categories used, that is 'affiliated adults' and 'adult members', although we would expect some similarity between them. Could it be that in ten years the Anglican Church has declined by almost 80 per cent?

Although it is generally accepted that there has been a decline in factors such as church attendance, we should be very cautious of assuming that this signifies that people no longer hold religious beliefs or identify with a particular church. Surveys have consistently shown that people identify with and feel themselves affiliated to churches. A survey in October 1982 by Gallup, commissioned by the Bible Society, revealed the extent of such affiliation.

Figure 7.5

Question: 'Which of the following, if any, is your religious denomination?'

		Percentage responding
1	Church of England	64
2	Roman Catholic	11
3	Methodist	7
4	Baptist	2
5	United Reformed	1
6	Jewish	
7	Moslem	1
8	Hindu	
9	Other	7
10	None	7

While the wording of the question may have influenced respondents and we may require details of the sampling and interview procedures to evaluate the results, they do suggest that many people continue to identify with a church and feel they have a 'religious denomination'. Again though, what this *means* is difficult to determine.

Studies of religious belief also indicate that religion is far from dead. In 1978 the EEC set up the 'European Values System Study Group' to explore a wide range of values and beliefs, including religious beliefs. This European survey involved 12,500 people in over twenty countries. In Britain the survey was carried out by Gallup, and involved a structured interview lasting about an hour. The following figures represent the replies of the British sample to three of the questions and provide interesting information concerning the extent of religious belief.

Figure 7.6

Question: 'Which, if any, of the following do you believe in?'

	%
God	76
Life after death	45
A soul	59
The devil	30
Sin	69
Hell	27
Heaven	57
Reincarnation	27

Figure 7.7

Question: 'Here are the ten Commandments. Please tell me if they still apply fully to yourself.'

		%
1	I am the Lord your God. You should have no other God before me	48
2	Thou shalt not take the name of the Lord thy God in vain	43
3	Thou shalt keep the Sabbath holy	25
4	Thou shalt honour thy father and mother	83
5	Thou shalt not kill	90
6	Thou shalt not commit adultery	78
7	Thou shalt not steal	87
8	Thou shalt not bear false witness against thy neighbour	78
9	Thou shalt not covet thy neighbours wife	79
10	Thou shalt not covet thy neighbours goods	79

A further survey by David Hay and colleagues at Nottingham University suggests that religious experiences are relatively common.

Figure 7.8

A further question asked the extent to which the respondents felt that others accepted the Commandment. A few examples suggested that the respondents felt few others did.

Commandment Number	Applies to Self %	Believe Others Accept It %
1	48	18
6	78	25
7	87	38
9	79	32
10	79	33

Reading 1   The spiritual experiences of the British

At a minimum, well over a third of all women and just under a third of all men in Great Britain claim to have had some sort of religious experience. By that I mean that they believe they have been aware of, or influenced by a presence or power, whether they call it God or not, which is different from their everyday selves. This was shown by a national survey conducted for us by National Opinion Polls in late 1976. The results are probably an under-statement of the true proportions, because it's asking a lot of somebody to talk about deeply personal experiences during the course of a short chat with an opinon pollstei.

In our most recent work, we've been carrying out lengthy interviews with a sample of adults in Nottingham and the positive response rate has gone up sharply, compared with the national sample. Because we have had time to build up rapport, we have managed to move beyond a taboo which nowadays is stronger than the one that stops people talking about their private sexual habits. . .

We've gathered a lot of information about the kinds of people who are most likely to talk about these things. On the whole, the more education they have, the more likely they are to claim experience. Of those who finished education at the age of 20 or beyond, 56 per cent said they'd had a religious experience, compared with 29 per cent of those who left school at 15. In a study of post-graduate students I did a few years ago, the positive response rate was 65 per cent. Another finding was that the middle class and middle-aged are more likely to claim experience than others. Just under a third of the people coming from unskilled and subsistance groups in the sample replied positively, compared with just under half of the middle glass group. Similarly, almost half of the people in the 65 plus age group said they'd been aware of a presence or power, compared with just under a third of those in the 16–24 age group.

Hay, D., 'The Spiritual Experiences of the British', *New Society*, 12th April, 1979.

What is also interesting about this research, however, is that almost half who claimed religious experiences never attended church, apart from weddings and funerals. David Hay suggests that although we are consistently told that we are living in a secular society, large numbers of people know they have had religious experiences – theories of religious decline must take account of these experiences.

8 Documentary readings

Civil religion

The concept of a civil religion has been defined in a number of ways but is generally accepted as being a set of beliefs and practices related to the past, present and future of a nation which are essentially 'sacred'. The concept is usually used by those who have adopted Durkheim's ideas to contemporary society. From his study of 'primitive' religions he argued that all societies needed regular events, ceremonies and rituals in order to reaffirm shared meanings and values. His argument suggests that there is little difference between specifically religious events such as Christmas (although it could be questioned how 'religious' this event is), and civil events such as American Independence Day or Thanksgiving, although even such events as these appear to have a religious quality. R. Bellah examined various aspects of civil religion, including presidential inaugural addresses, and found considerable references to religion. President Kennedy's inaugural address ended with the following statement:

> with a good conscience our only sure reward, with history the final judge of our deeds, let us go forth to lead the land we love, asking His blessing and His help, but knowing that here on earth God's work must truly be our own.

In the following extract McGuire gives further examples of America's civil religion.

Reading 2   American civil religion

Many American civil ceremonies have a marked religious quality. Memorial Day, Fourth of July, presidential inaugurations, all celebrate national values and national unity. There are national shrines such as the memorials in Washington,

D.C., the Capital itself, the birthplace of key presidents, war memorials, and other 'special' places. It is not their age or even historical significance but their ability to symbolise transcendence of the nation as a 'people' that inspires awe and reverence. A visitor to Independence Hall said, 'Just standing here sends chills down my spine.' National shrines are 'sacred' in Durkheim's sense of the word. Likewise there are sacred objects of the civil religion – especially the flag. Interestingly the Bible is probably also a sacred object in civil religion, not because of its content but because it signifies an appeal to God as the ultimate arbiter of truth and justice. The extent to which these ceremonies, shrines, and objects are set apart as sacred can be seen in the intensity of outrage at inappropriate behaviour or 'desecration'. Some people were arrested during the 1960s for wearing or displaying a copy of the American flag improperly (e.g., on the seat of their pants).

American civil religion also has its myths and saints. Lincoln is a historical figure who particularly symbolises the civil religion. His actions and speeches contributed to the articulation of that religion in a time of crisis, and his life from his humble birth to his martyrdom typifies values of the civil religion. Other 'saints' include key presidents (Washington, Jefferson, Wilson, Franklin D. Roosevelt, Kennedy), folk heroes (Davy Crockett, Charles A. Lindberg), and military heroes (MacArthur, Eisenhower, Theodore Roosevelt). Similarly there are stories that exemplify valued traits (e.g., the Horatio Alger rags-to-riches genre) and images (the frontier). Socially important myths include the American Dream – the land of plenty – unlimited social mobility, economic consumption, and achievement. While these shrines, saints, and ceremonies are not religious in the same sense as, for example, Greek Orthodox shrines, saints, and ceremonies, they are still set apart as special and not to be profaned.

McGuire, M. B., Religion: The social context,
Wadsworth Publishing Co., California, 1981.

While much of the work on civil religion has been tied to the American context, some attempt has been made to apply it to this country. The most notable of these attempts was probably that by Shils and Young. They begin their analysis of the Coronation by arguing that in all societies there exists fundamental agreement over moral standards and beliefs. Such

values as generosity, loyalty, respect for authority and the dignity
of the individual enable society to hold itself together. These
values are given a sacred status, which when symbolised and
reinforced in ritual activities increases their effectiveness. In the
following extracts the authors continue their argument, showing
the importance of Durkheim for their analysis.

Reading 3   English civil religion: the Coronation

If this argument be accepted, it is barely necessary to state the
interpretation of the Coronation which follows from it: that
the Coronation was the ceremonial occasion for the affirma-
tion of the moral values by which the society lives. It was an act
of national communion. In this we are merely restating the
interpretation, in a particular context, of a more general view
(which can apply to Christmas, Independence Day, Thanksgiving Day, May Day, or any other great communal ritual)
expressed by a great sociologist. (Durkheim).

The Coronation is exactly this kind of ceremonial in which
the society reaffirms the moral values which constitute it as a
society and renews its devotion to those values by an act of
communion.

Just as the Coronation service in the Abbey was a religious
ceremony in the conventional sense, so then the popular
participation in the service throughout the country had many
of the properties of the enactment of a religious ritual. For one
thing, it was not just an extraordinary spectacle, which people
were interested in as individuals in search of enjoyment. The
Coronation was throughout a collective, not an individual
experience.

The greatly increased sensitivity of individuals to their social
ties, the greater absorption of the individual into his group and
therewith into the larger community through his group found
expression not only on the procession route but in the absent
people as well, notably through their families. The family,
despite the ravages of urban life and despite those who allege
that it is in dissolution, remains one of the most sinewy of
institutions. The family tie is regarded as sacred, even by those
who would or do, shirk the diffuse obligations it imposes. The
Coronation, like any other great occasion which in some
manner touches the sense of the sacred, brings vitality into

family relationships. The Coronation, much like Christmas, was a time for drawing closer the bonds of the family, for re-asserting its solidarity and for re-emphasising the values of the family – generosity, loyalty, love – which are at the same time the fundamental values necessary for the well being of the larger society.

The Coronation provided at one time and for practically the entire society such an intensive contact with the sacred that we believe we are justified in interpreting it as we have done in this essay, as a great act of national communion.

Shils, E., and Young, M., The meaning of the coronation, *Sociological Review*, 1953.

Although Shils and Young focused our attention on Durkheim's interpretation of religion as reaffirming societies values, it has been heavily criticised, especially from a Marxist perspective, Birnbaum's article, which appeared two years later, not only served to give a Marxist interpretation of the events connected with the Coronation, but also to show how religious activities can be interpreted in a variety of ways. After summarising the argument of Shils and Young, Birnbaum offers an alternative interpretation:

Reading 4   Marxist view of the Coronation

Another argument might run this way. The very absence of shared values in Great Britain accounts for some of the attention paid to the Coronation. The Coronation provided, for some sections of the populace, some measure of the surcease from that condition of conflict which is more or less permanent for complex societies, of an industrial and capitalist type. Under this viewpoint, the role of the press in stirring up popular enthusiasm for the Coronation is less inexplicable. In response to the class interests it generally represents, the press continually seeks to minimise awareness of the real conflicts characteristic of British Society. But the Coronation was a holiday, and its connections with the daily routine of social relationships was by no means as critical as the authors imagine. In this context, the personality of the Queen and her family functioned as the object of various fantasies and identifications in a way not much more 'sacred' than the cult of

adulation built up around certain film stars.'
> Birnbaum, N., 'Monarchs and sociologists',
> *Sociological Review*, 1955.

Attempts have also been made to see the concept of civil religion as a form of nationalism, or nation building. Thus a nationalistic or civil religion can bring diverse groups together in a central and unifying experience. McGuire argues that:

Reading 5   Nationalism and civil religion

This nation building potential can be seen in the attempts to develop an Arab civil religion in the Middle East. Lacking an Islamic tradition of effective political participation, some Arabs are consciously trying to develop Islam into a national (i.e. civil) religion. They present Muhammed as an Arab hero whose convictions inspired him to initiate a new civilization, create an Arab culture and unifying the Arab peoples.
> McGuire, 1981.

While the concept of civil religion may help us to understand the ways in which the individual is integrated into wider society, it is clear that it is open to a number of criticisms. From a Marxist perspective, and as Birnbaum's criticism of Shils and Young implied, such a concept does not confront the possibility that religious beliefs may be ideologies which serve to legitimate domination and passify the subordinate. Furthermore, there is a danger that in stressing the effects of a civil religion in holding society together other variables which have an integrative role, such as economic dependence, are largely ignored. Bryan Turner offers two other difficulties with the concept, the first being the problems of 'rituals' which for those who adopt Durkheim's perspective is important for social integration.

Reading 6   Criticism of the concept of civil religion

The concept of 'ritual' as any regular, repetitive, standardised activity of a non–utilitarian character is thus broad enough to embrace the most diverse collection of activities from changing the guard at Buckingham Palace to Memorial Day, from the opening of Parliament to saluting the flag. There is, in principle, no method of restricting the list of rituals which could count as part of the civil religion; unfortunately the diversity of the examples does not appear to carry any theoretical embarrassment for advocates of the efficacy of civil religions. Given the vagueness of the concept it would indeed be difficult to know what to exclude. The civil religion argument does suffer from a common methodological difficulty which it shares with all arguments relating to the notion of a dominant culture. It equates social prevalence with cultural dominance, confusing frequency with social effects. A strong thesis about a dominant culture or civil religion would have to show that the beliefs and practices in question played a necessary part in the maintenance and continuity of a social system. It cannot be assumed that beliefs and practices which are publicly available necessarily have significant effects in the upkeep of crucial social processes and social arrangements. Most civil religion arguments concerning nationalism are weak theories which point to the presence of certain allegedly common practices and suggest that these have integrative consequences. With respect to such ceremonies as the Royal Wedding, Independence Day celebrations, or the Coronation, one can show that these have social effects in the trivial sense that people are involved in them at various levels, but one has to go further to demonstrate that these rituals have specific effects on the stablility of capitalist society. From the existence of communal rituals, one cannot make the assumption that these are functionally necessary or that they perform the functions ascribed to them. On existing evidence, the civil religion is at best loosely and only periodically connected with the reactivation of a problematic conscience collective, but the precise connections between these common sentiments and the structural arrangements of industrial society is inadequately specified.

Turner, B. S., *Religion and Social Theory*, Heinemann Educational Books, London, 1983.

Questions

1 Using the extract from McGuire as an example, make a list of similar features of Britain's 'civil' religion.

2 Using Birnbaum's criticisms of the work by Shils and Young, employ a similar critique of the notion of a civil religion exmployed by McGuire.

3 Does the concept of civil religion offer any insights into the secularisation debate?

4 Given the criticisms of civil religion which have been outlined and some examples of the way it has been employed, how useful is the concept for understanding religion in contemporary societies?

Secularisation

Secularisation is a broad concept which, as we have seen, has been interpreted in a variety of ways. In this series of extracts we shall briefly look at two interpretations of the present role of religion in modern industrial societies and then turn to various problems associated with secularisation. In particular we shall look at what some sociologists have referred to as the 'myth' of secularisation.

For Bryan Wilson secularisation is a broad concept which covers a wide variety of aspects:

Reading 7   The secularisation of religion

Secularisation relates to the diminution in the social significance of religion. Its application covers such things as, the sequestration by political powers of the property and facilities of religious agencies; the shift from religious to secular control of the various erstwhile activities and functions of religion; the decline in the proportion of their time, energy and resources which men devote to super-empirical concerns; the decay of religious institutions; the supplanting, in matters of behaviour, of religious precepts by demands that accord with strictly technical criteria; and the gradual replacement of a specifically religious consciousness (which might range from dependence on charms, rites, spells or prayers, to a broadly spiritually-inspired ethical concern) by an empirical, rational, instrumental orientation; the abandonment of mythical, poetic, and artistic interpretations of nature and society in favour of matter-of-fact description and, with it, the rigorous separation of evaluative and emotive dispositions from cognitive and positivistic orientations.

Wilson, B., *Religion in Sociological Perspective*,
Oxford University Press, Oxford, 1982.

Wilson links the process of secularisation to the process of 'societalisation' – the movement away from organisation based on the local community to the large scale society. For him this process of secularisation is well documented and self evident, and as such it becomes important to focus on the consequences and implications for society. These consequences range from increased social disorder to a threat to Western civilisation itself:

Reading 8   The consequences of secularisation

At present, in the West, the remnants of religion are, if receding, as yet still in evidence, but generally it may be said that western culture lives off the borrowed capital of its religious past. It is by no means clear what sort of society is coming into being as religious values wane. The consequences, not only for the arts and for high culture, but also, and perhaps more importantly, for the standards of civic order, social responsibility, and individual integrity, may be such that the future of western civilisation itself may be thrown into jeopardy. To opine that these effects might ensue, is not, of course, to imply that the particular religious values of western society were in any sense either intrinsically warranted or specifically necessary for the maintenance of civilised order. It is, rather, to suggest that at least in western society the functions that were in the past supplied by, or at least supported by, religion, may now be left unserviced, and so to raise the question of whether in the future the conditions of life will ever be wholly humane without the operation of some such agencies.

Wilson, 1982.

While Wilson's style and argument may have much appeal, it does raise a number of problems and questions. Firstly, is society any less stable than in the past? Has social disorder increased, and if it has is this due to the process of secularisation or are other factors involved? Secondly, although Wilson outlines a process of societalisation in which efficiency and rationality predominate, he never seems to ask the question 'In whose interests do these operate?' A third problem concerns whether the processes are as negative as Wilson suggests. Does the growth of alternative meaning systèms at least provide choice? Finally we might expect, having outlined the problems involved, at least some discussion of possible solutions; a return perhaps to traditional religion, or will society inevitably follow the road to increased social disorder and disintegration?

Although Wilson claims to offer some evidence of the decline in the social significance of religion, and begins to question the consequences, others have argued that religion still provides important services and that religious values are not far from the surface:

Reading 9   The survival of religion

In the first place, religious bodies are the largest voluntary agencies in the country, and therefore on any reckoning make a massive contribution to the richness of institutional life, and to the social training and support of individuals.

Secondly, they nurture, both directly and indirectly, many of the values and general attitudes on which the conduct of public life depends, not least in their ability to challenge and disturb, as well as to heal and restore. It is not claimed that the churches are the sole source of such values, only that they are an important source, and that some important values seem to belong particularly within a religious context.

Thirdly, religion meets the need for a public language of hope, aspiration, penitence and renewal even though the particular languages of particular religious bodies are no longer fully accessible to more than a minority.

Fourthly, Britain has maintained a formal public commitment to the Christian faith, expressed in part through the Monarchy. . .

Fifthly. . . there is a specific Christian contribution to be made towards the understanding and attainment of unity.

> Habgood, J., *Church and Nation in a Secular Age*,
> Darton, Longman and Todd, London, 1983.

While Wilson's interpretation is one of decline, Habgood points to the continual significance of religion. Both however, appear to adopt a definition of religion in institutional terms, which may not surprise us given the predominance of what is usually referred to as positivist sociology. This approach assumes that only what is directly observable can be studied, and that aspects such as motives and feelings which are not directly observable may be misleading and relatively unimportant. Hence sociologists' attempts to have their findings given 'scientific status' has frequently led to a concern with positivist methods. We might also add that another factor encouraging the use of positivist methods of research has been the influence of those who employ the researchers. The churches have tended to be interested in secularisation in institutional terms.

Luckmann outlines some of the consequences of this approach:

Reading 10   Church and religion

The main assumption – which also has the most important consequences for research and theory in the sociology of religion – consists in the identification of church and religion. On occasion this assumption is explicitly formulated as a methodological principle: religion may be many things, but it is amenable to scientific analysis only to the extent that it becomes organised and institutionalised. Most other assumptions are intimately linked with this main assumption or are directly derived from it. Religion becomes a social fact either as ritual (institutionalised religious conduct) or doctrine (institutionalised religious ideas).

The identification of church and religion fits into the dominant view of sociology as the science of social institutions – the latter term understood narrowly. It is also congruent with theoretical positivism. In the traditional positivist view religion is the institutional conglomerate of certain irrational beliefs.

Vestiges of this view have entered the understanding – or misunderstanding – of secularisation and characterises much – of the recent sociology of religion. In the absence of a well-founded theory, secularisation is typically regarded as a process of religious pathology to be measured by the shrinking reach of the churches. Since the institutional vacuum is not being filled by a counter-church. . . one readily concludes that modern society is nonreligious. . . . The churches remain, in a manner of speaking, islands of religion (or irrationality) in a sea of secularism (or reason). It only remains for the sociologist of religion to analyse the national and class differences in the process of religious decline – that is, of the shrinking reach of the churches. Under these circumstances it need surprise no one that the historical and ethnological horizons of the recent sociology of religion are, on the whole extremely narrow.

Luckmann, T., *The Invisible Religion*, Collier–Macmillan, London, 1967.

Defining secularisation in these terms then, can be seen as a consequence of a dominant view of what sociology is and how it should go about research. Many however, have criticised this method of research and its definition of religion in institutional terms. For Luckmann such research has led to the development of a myth – the myth of secularisation:

Reading 11   The myth of secularisation?

I begin by stating my assumptions. I think that the notion of secularisation offers a largely fictitious account of the transformations of religion in Western society during the past centuries. In consequence it camouflages the nature of religion in the contemporary world. To the extent that secularisation is a myth rather than a reasonably objective sociological or historical construct, it misdirects our observations of religion as a social reality in late industrial society. I shall try to substantiate this assertion. The sociology of religion was and still is preoccupied by the problem of secularisation or what it considers to be that problem. The problem is generally defined in the following fashion. Sociology is a science of social institutions. Religion becomes amenable to sociological analysis in so far as it is organised in social institutions. For all practical purposes, religion as a social fact is to be found in churches, sects and in the attitudes determined by them. As a result of a rather mysterious process, generally attributed in some fashion to social and cultural change, religious institutions in industrial societies seem to have less influence on the conduct and the attitudes of the population or, at any rate, of significant groups and strata in the population, than they presumably had in earlier times. Empirical research shows that specifically religious attitudes i.e. attitudes defined by the norms of religious institutions, have either become marginal in industrial society as, for example, in Europe or where penetrated by traditionally non-religious values, as in the United States. Modern society is, therefore, fundamentally secular. This 'theory' is shaky and its operationalisations in research are simple–minded.

> Luckmann, T., *Life-World and Social Realities*, Heinemann Educational Books, London, 1983.

Peter Glasner in his critique of the concept of secularisation also provides us with possible causes of the development of the secularisation 'myth'. His book can be seen not only as a criticism of secularisation, but of much contemporary research. He argues that surrounding the concept has been a belief that in the past there was a golden age of religion, but that there has been a steady progress towards some rational, secular society. It has also been assumed that this process has been evenly spread throughout society and the industrialised world. He supports Luckmann's argument that there has been an uncritical use of conventional definitions of religion which has affected the research tools adopted and the conclusions reached.

In this extract he summarises his general criticisms of the secularisation 'myth'.

Reading 12   Glasner on the secularisation myth

This discussion has, therefore, been an attack on contemporary sociology in several ways; it has suggested the ubiquity of the ideology of progress in sociologists' views of the place of religion in society; it has argued that this ideology has been promoted through the use of a particular methodology; it has suggested that a major ordering concept, secularisation, has become a sociological myth (and that, by implication, it may not be alone); and finally it has suggested that there is little by way of scientific theory to help conceptualise the understanding of the secularisation process.

Hence 'theories' of the secularisation process become social

myths through their reliance on systematic empiricism.
Glasner, P. E., *The Sociology of Secularisation*,
Routledge and Kegan Paul, London, 1977.

A further difficulty with secularisation is that there are various levels of analysis. Glasner points to the interpersonal, organisational, and the cultural levels. While Luckmann and others appear willing to accept the idea that on an organisational level society has become secularised, on an individual level this is not the case: 'The social structure is secularised – but the myth of secularisation fails to account for the fact that the individual is not secularised.' (Luckmann, T., 1983).

Given such criticisms we are left with the problem of whether the term secularisation has any value. I suspect that it does, but only if it is carefully defined and analysed at various levels. In this way adopting an exclusive definition of religion (one which excludes other belief systems such as Marxism), and analysing at an organisational level, it may be possible to refer to a process towards secularisation. If, however, we adopt an inclusive definition of religion and analyse at the individual level then it may not be possible to identify such a process. Even here though, and as Chapter 3 showed, there is considerable controversy and debate. Such debate, while showing the difficulties and problems which sociologists face, also points to its vitality and interest as we attempt to come to terms with and understand society and social processes.

Discussion questions

1 Is it significant that while Bryan Wilson writes as a Reader in Sociology in the University of Oxford, John Habgood writes as Archbishop of York?
2 Religion has been defined by many in institutional terms. How else could it be defined, and in what ways might this affect the methods used and the conclusions arrived at?
3 Look carefully at the problems and questions concerning Reading 8. How would you answer them?
4 How might different sociologists criticise and question Habgood's arguments?
5 Given the wide variety of meaning attached to the term secularisation, is it worth keeping?

The Protestant Ethic thesis

Every few years the debate concerning the role of Calvinism in the development of capitalism rears its head. In part the debate concerns new historical insights and new applications of the theory to other countries. However, it remains central to sociology since it raises questions not only about the relationship between religious beliefs and economic action, but the significance of changes in the religious dimension on society as a whole.

In the following readings we shall briefly explore some of the criticisms and defences of Weber's argument. The first extract is drawn from Eisenstadt's useful summary of the debates concerning Weber's thesis. He provides a brief outline of some of the early criticisms:

Reading 13   Weber's thesis: early criticisms

> It was often stressed that the first great upsurges of capitalism developed in pre-Reformation Catholic Europe – be it Italy, Belgium or Germany – and that they were much more 'developed' that those in the first Protestant or Calvinist countries. On the contrary, economic retrogression or retardation very often set in in many of these communities, as for instance in Calvin's Geneva, to no small degree due to the restrictive orientations of the Protestant communities. . .
> Eisenstadt, S. N., 'The Protestant Ethic thesis in analystical and comparative context', *Diogenes*, 59, 1967.

A further extract from Robertson shows how the connection between Calvinism and capitalism becomes a 'chicken and egg' argument – did Calvinism cause capitalism, or did capitalism cause Calvinism. The debate is thus between those who argue that ideas can lead to economic change, and those who argue that economic change leads to changes in ideas and beliefs. Robertson argues that there was nothing exceptional in Calvinist teachings and many of the beliefs which Weber attributed to Calvinists were shared by Catholics and others. Furthermore, many of the doctrines to which Weber attached great importance such as predestination, only spread at the end of the seventeenth century, by which time the spirit of capitalism was well developed.

Reading 14   Weber's thesis: cause or effect?

It would appear that this is in itself enough to prove that the problem has been viewed through the wrong end of the telescope – to show that the chief relation between the rise of the capitalist spirit and the Protestant Ethic is the reverse of what Weber indicated. The Protestant Ethic changed as the result of the influence of a rising capitalistically-minded middle class.'

Robertson, H. M., in Green R. W., (ed), *Protestantism and Capitalism*, Heath and Co., Boston, USA, 1959.

We should remember however, that Weber's Protestant Ethic thesis was only a small part of his work on religion and capitalism. Many of his writings on comparative religions were attempts to show that other religions did not have the same affinity with the capitalist spirit that Calvinism had. This approach however, has also been criticised:

Reading 15   Comparative perspectives

There is nothing to indicate. . . that the Muslim religion prevented the Muslim world from developing along the road to modern capitalism, any more than there is anything to indicate that Christianity directed the Western European world along that road. Islam did not prescribe to or impose upon the people, the civilisation, the states that adopted its teachings any specific economic road.'

Rodinson, M., *Islam and Capitalism*, Penguin Books, Harmondsworth, Middlesex, 1980.

Many of the criticisms rely on various historical chronologies – the times at which Calvinism and capitalism are said to have developed. While these criticisms are clearly a problem for Weber's thesis there have been attempts to support him. For example, Gordon Marshall explains why capitalism failed to develop in Scotland as successfully as it did in England:

Reading 16   Scotland and capitalism

Scots capitalists did not lack appropriate motivation to 'capitalist accumulation' but their designs were for more than a century, frustrated by the backwardness of the economic structure of the country, in other words by the conditions of action that circumscribed their activities. Under these circumstances, the modern capitalist economy was relatively slow to develop in Scotland, but this is precisely what Weber himself would have predicted.'

Marshall, G., *Presbyteries and Profits*, Clarendon Press, Oxford, 1980.

While the debate over Weber's Protestant Ethic thesis continues to rage, others have explored different forms of religion and their consequences for social change. Gary Marx, for example, has explored the question of whether religion can be seen as either an 'opiate' or 'inspiration' of civil rights movements amongst blacks in America. Although his investigation is narrower than exploring religion and change generally, his analysis once again warns us of making generalisations about all religions. While 'other-worldly' religions may inhibit protest, 'this-worldly' orientations, or what he terms 'temporal', do not.

Reading 17   Religion and race

The effect of religiosity on race protest depends on the type of religiosity involved. Past literature is rich in suggestions that the religiosity of the fundamentalist sects is an alternative to the development of political radicalism. This seems true in the case of race protest as well. However, in an overall sense even those who belong to the more conventional churches, the greater the religious involvement, whether measured in terms of ritual activity, orthodoxy of religious belief, subjective importance of religion, or all three taken together, the lower the degree of militancy.

Among sect members and religious people with an other-worldly orientation, religion and race protest appear to be, if not mutually exclusive, then certainly what one observer has referred as as 'mutually corrosive kinds of commitments.' Until such time as religion loosens its hold over these people or comes to embody to a greater extent the belief that man as well as God can bring about secular change, and focuses more on the here and how, religious involvement may be seen as an important factor working against the widespread radicalisation of the Negro public.

However, it has also been noted that many militant people are nevertheless religious. When a distinction is made among the religious between the 'otherwordly' and the 'temporal', for many of the latter group, religion seems to facilitate or at least not inhibit protest. For these people religion and race protest may be mutually supportive.'

Marx, G. T., 'Religion: opiate or inspiration of civil rights militancy among negroes', *American Sociological Review*, 32, 1967.

It has often been argued that Marx gave religion a far more conservative role than Weber. During industrialisation especially it was, and is, widely assumed that religion served to keep the working classes quiet and conformist. Robert Tressell's novel about his observations on a group of painters and decorators in Hastings around 1906 gives some insights into this aspect, and serves as a powerful reminder of Marxist analysis.

The extract concerns a conversation between a young boy, Frankie, and his Mother.

Reading 18   *The Ragged Trousered Philanthropists*

'Well the vicar goes about telling the Idlers that it's quite right for them to do nothing, and that God meant them to have nearly everything that is made by those who work. In fact he tells them that God made the poor for the use of the rich. Then he goes to the workers and tells them that God meant them to work very hard and to give all the good things they make to those who do nothing, and that they should be very thankful to God and to the Idlers for being allowed to have even the very worst food to eat and the rags and broken boots to wear. He also tells them that they mustn't grumble, or be discontented because they're poor in this world, but that they must wait till they're dead, and then God will reward them by letting them go to a place called heaven.'

Frankie laughed.

'And what about the Idlers?' he asked.

'The vicar says that if they believe everything he tells them and give him some of the money they make out of the workers, then God will let them into heaven also.' . . .

'And what about the workers? Do they believe it?'

'Most of them do, because when they were little children like you, their mothers taught them to believe, without thinking, whatever the vicar said, and that God made them for the use of the Idlers. When they went to school, they were taught the same thing: and now they've grown up they really believe it, and they go to work and give nearly everything they make to the Idlers, and have next to nothing left for themselves and their children. That's the reason why the Idlers and their children have more clothes than they need and more food than they can eat. Some of them have so many clothes that they are not able to wear them and so much food that they are not able to eat it. They just waste it or throw it away.'

Tressell, R., *The Ragged Trousered Philanthropists*,
Granada Publishing, London, 1965.

Although Tressell's novel provides an example of the way in which religion may justify, legitimate and hide the real basis of inequality, it would not be accurate to assume that this is true of all religions.

Parkin's work, which is concerned with the exploitative relationship between dominant and subordinate classes and the problem of social control, points out that not all religions can be seen as a 'prop to inequality':

Reading 19   Religion and social control

Again the view of religion as a prop to inequality and political converservatism would not accurately portray the activities of all churches in all societies. Occasionally the Church and its leaders have been at the spearhead of movements aimed at improving the condition of the underclass. In the southern United States, for example, political leadership among the Negro population has frequently been assumed by clergymen, and the churches have tended to provide an organisational focus for the civil rights campaign. This has partly to do with the fact that Negro political organisations were not easily established in the repressive conditions of the southern states, so that the churches became natural rallying points in the struggle against inequality. The evidence here suggests that religious institutions can themselves be politically radicalised under certain conditions – especially perhaps where there are no other formal political outlets for the expression of material grievances. Protestant churches have sometimes played a similar role on behalf of Africans in part of white-dominated Africa, while the Catholic Church in Eastern Europe has often been one major focus of political opposition to communist governments.

Parkin, F., *Class Inequality and Political Order,* Paladin,
St Albans, 1972.

Parkin's work however, does not provide us with a general theoretical model which would allow us to explain and examine the complex relationship between religion and social change. Such a comprehensive theory is noticeable in its absence, especially when both concepts of change and religion are central to sociology. This point is made by Thomas Luckmann:

Reading 20   Religion and social change

There are no theories of religion in relation to social change. Even if one were to adopt the far less stringent understanding of the term that is current in the social sciences, there would be little to report. If one wanted to take everything that has a bearing on the problem, however, few ideas in sociology and anthropology should be left out of the catalogue. This is not very surprising. The notion of social change and the notion of religion are key categories in most attempts to understand human affairs. But they are as elusive and vague as they are important and ubiquitous. In many contexts the notions are used to good advantage and everyone seems to know what one is talking about. But attempts to define precisely either concept leave the ordinary reader baffled, and infuriate fellow scholars.

Luckmann, T., 1983.

Where do we go from here? Luckmann takes the view that the

development of a completely theory of the relationship between religion and social change is riddled with insurmountable problems. Not only do we require a general agreement on what is meant by change and religion, but we also require a theory which will take into account the wide variety of forms these phenomena take, as well as the complex interrelations between them. While we wait for such a development it seems appropriate to attempt to begin to outline some aspects which may have a bearing on the relationship. The extracts from Gary Marx and Frank Parkin have both indicated possible directions of analysis.

Questions

1 How would Weber combat the criticisms of his thesis outlined in Readings 13, 14 and 15?
2 Why would Weber have predicted that capitalism would be slow to develop in Scotland?
3 What characteristics do Gary Marx and Frank Parkin point to which might help explain why religion is sometimes an agent of social change and not at other times? Can you add any others?
4 How might the secularisation debate challenge the observations of Tressell if they were made today?

Religious sects

Many sociologists agree that society has undergone considerable change over the years. This change is characterised by a growth of the State and bureaucratic regulation, the decline of established integrated communities and the growth of alternative ways of looking at the world. Many see these changes as presenting people with a crisis. As old values begin to be challenged there is a crisis of meaning, of identity and purpose.

In such a situation sects may serve to provide a coherent set of values within a well established and integrated community, which offers both hope for the future and a goal in life. One example of such a movement is the Black Muslims. Not only does the movement offer a means of communicating the blacks' sense of frustration and anger at the inequalities, discrimination and limited life chances which American society is seen as offering them, but it also provides cohesion and a sense of belonging. The following short extract from Howard Kaplan provides some examples of what the movement can offer its members:

Reading 21   Joining the Black Muslims

It offers him a REBIRTH. He can shed his old despised identity. It offers him an emotional if not physical OUTLET for his newly articulated hostility toward the white man. It offers him HOPE. Joining the highly moralistic and disciplined Black Muslims gives him the immanent prospect of raising himself from his debilitating condition of poverty and frustration. It also provides him with the GOAL of building for a new glorious future in a united and powerful black society.

> Kaplan, H. M., 'The Black Muslims and the Negro
> American's quest for communion',
> British Journal of Sociology, 20, June 1969.

Bryan Wilson on the other hand sees these new sects in a very different light. For him society has become increasingly differentiated and divided. Unlike religion in the past which served to integrate society and provided a sense of moral cohesion, these sects tend to take the individual out of society and aid the process of division and disunity:

Reading 22   Wilson on religious cults

They have no real consequence for other social institutions, for political power structures, for technological constraints and controls. They add nothing to any prospective reintegration of society, and contribute nothing towards the culture by which society might live.

The religious revivals of earlier times were not of this kind. They had significant social consequenes. They occurred in societies with basic units of much smaller scale, when the diffusion of new dispositions, and the inculcation of new attitudes were vital adjuncts in the process of social change, as in the Third World they may be still. The West, in contrast, appears to have passed beyond the point at which religious teaching and practice can exercise formative influence over whole societies, or any significant segment of them. The new cults cannot be compared with Methodism, which some scholars have regarded as so important that they credit it with the prevention in England of the equivalent of the French Revolution. Methodism arose at a time when society was still largely regulated by personal relationships, and could thus affect social structure by mobilising individual dispositions. What it accomplished was a massive gentling of the people: new values were communicated, and standards of disinterested goodwill were steadily diffused through a much wider body of the population.

Wilson goes on to argue that:

They pronounce their distrust of the scientific routinsed, and bureaucratic procedures on which modern social systems depend, and demand a rediscovery of the self by avenues of exploration previously forbidden. But whereas earlier religious revivals, revivalism within a religious tradition, led to a reintegration of the individual within the social order, the new cults propose to take the individual out of society, and to save him by the wisdom of some other, wholly exotic body of belief and practice.

The new cults do not serve society. They are indeed almost irrelevant to it, since their sources of inspiration are exotic, esoteric, subjective, and subterranean. Truth comes from far places, or from lower social strata, or from hitherto untapped depths of the self or the psyche. Thus, conceptions of socially inspired self-restraint, and coordination of individuals within the wider society, on which all ongoing social systems depend, are entirely alien. Instead of restraint there is an emphasis on pleasure.

Wilson, B., *Contemporary Transformations of Religion,*
Clarendon Press, Oxford, 1976.

While Wilson appears to see these movements as irrelevant or inconsequential, he nevertheless condemns them wholeheartedly. A very different view, however, is provided by Glock and Bellah who suggest that sects are an indication of a new awareness and spiritual sensitivity. Like Wilson they seem to see them as a protest against national and international violence, poverty, racial strife and the problem of meaning. Unlike Wilson however, they suggest that these religious movements may serve to reintegrate some into society and provide beneficial social functions.

Reading 23   Sects and social integration

They have provided a stable social setting and a coherent set of symbols for young people disorientated by the drug culture or disillusioned with radical politics. What Synanon claims to have done for hard-core drug users, religious groups – from Zen Buddhists to Jesus people – have done for ex-hippes. . . In many instances reconciliation with parents has been facilitated by the more stable life-style and the religious ideology of acceptance rather than confrontation. A new, more positive orientation toward occupational roles has often developed. In some cases such as followers of Meher Baba, this has meant a return to school and the resumption of a normal middle-class career pattern. For others, such as resident devotees of the San Francisco Zen Centre or ashram residents of the 3HO movement, jobs are seen largely as means to subsistence, having little value in themselves. While the attitude toward work in terms of punctuality, thoroughness, and politeness is, from the employer's point of view, positive, the religious devotee has no inner commitment to the job nor does he look forward to any advancement.

Bellah, R. N., in Glock, C. Y., and Bellah, R. N. (eds.), *The New Religious Consciousness*, University of California Press, Berkeley, 1976.

A similar theme is developed by Gregory Johnson who analysed the Hare Krishna movement in San Francisco. Although, like Glock and Bellah, he sees the movement as serving to realign its members with society, he argues that on an individual level they still rejected it. Although in the past this had often been in the form of a refusal to participate in society and to 'drop out' into the world of drugs, the new rejection was an acknowledgement that society was simply unworthy of any concern. Although they might remain in the world, they were not of the world.

Reading 24   The Hare Krishna movement

The movement seemed to realign its members with the moral imperatives of the larger society. The behaviour of the initiates was drastically changed: they forsook many of their previous activities (some viewed by society as illegal or questionable) and lived an ascetic life. In some ways, theirs was a model life. They abstained from drugs, alcohol, cigarettes, and sex. They cut their previously long hair and kept it short when it grew back. The conservative, world-acceptance teachings of the Gita led to a resolution of personal disputes with society. Employment for instance, was no longer a sellout. The previously deviant life-style was channeled into different directions, which were no longer illegal but merely strange, amusing, or perplexing. They could not easily be placed in a category (such as 'hippie') by the public at large. . . The devotees were immune from formal societal sanction because illegal drugs had been renounced. In this sense, they could be compared to a drug-rehabilitation organisation, such as Synanon, in which the members also cut their hair, became isolated from the outside world, and practiced rigid adherence to certain rules. But the comparison was not complete, because only the members outwardly deviant behaviour was changed: practicing Krishna Consciousness, the members frequently explained, was a way to stay 'high' all the time. . . .
Did the movement reaffirm the individual's pre-existing deviant life-style? Or did it reconcile the individual with society?
On the surface the latter alternative seemed feasible. Some members secured employment, ceased to be concerned with changing the social order, and renounced illegal drugs. From the standpoint of the larger society, these people were no longer factors of instablity and were contributing more productively. At the level of the individual, however, it would seem that personal alienation had not decreased. In Weber's terms, the person was 'in the world' but not 'of the world'. Disaffection from the larger society was merely reaffirmed and revitalised in a different symbolic package. . . The members had already rejected traditional life patterns when they entered Krishna Consciouness. The movement idealised, organised, and dogmatised many of the members' previous hippie attitudes. This represents a threshold in an alienating process. The individual was no longer merely personally disaffected by

existing society – he refused to believe it worthy of his attention.

Johnson, G., in Glock, C. Y. and Bellah, R. N., 1976.

The debate over whether sects can have integrative functions is important. In many ways it can be seen in relation to Durkheim's problem of order and social cohesion. Whereas some seem to suggest that sects might play a useful role in integrating people back into wider society and re-establishing society's values, others see this as an idealistic intepretation. In part this reflects the difficulties of making any generalisations about all sects, and the need for us to distinguish between different types.

David Gordon, who spent two years observing, participating in, and carrying out interviews in two Jesus People groups in a city in the United States, found significant differences between them. In the first (JPU), which was a commune of 90 members, the community operated to separate the convert from the world and former ties, whereas the second (JPS), a non-communal group of 30, the religious community operated to reintegrate the convert into the world and with his social ties.

Gordon found a number of similarities between the two groups. Both were fundamentalist Christian groups who believed in the literal truth of the Bible, and that the highest service to an individual was to help them accept Jesus. Both groups were founded by evangelistic individuals and had similar membership in terms of age (average 21 years), education and socio-economic status. Gordon argues that it is largely the previous relationship of the members to society which will determine whether the group will integrate or not.

Reading 25   Gordon on Jesus People

The major difference between the two groups. . . is in the area of relationships with others, especially families. The JPU encourages members to establish relationships within the group while the JPS encourages members to retain relationships with those outside the group.

Two possible explanations can be given for these differences between the two Jesus People groups. On the one hand the members of the groups could self-select themselves on the basis of whether or not their ties with family and other lines of activity had already been broken. On the other hand the groups themselves could be responsible for either breaking or reinforcing these ties. On the basis of the interviews with members of both groups both explanations seem to hold with the first being most important. . .

The common elements which emerge from the JPU interviews are a loss of a parent through death or divorce, antagonistic relationships with parents, an adolescent reputation as a promiscuous or bad person, as an outcast or loner, heavy drinking and/or drug use, a period of separation from the family preceding involvement with the JPU, and a search for order and acceptance. The few exceptions to this pattern joined the JPU as the result of having close friends or siblings who joined ahead of them.

Those who joined the JPS typically had not left home, jobs or school, but were having difficulties with their parents. Joining the JPS often made things worse for a time, but the group's belief in submission to parents eventually led to a reconciliation with at least one parent and usually with both. In this case the group functions to adjust relationships between members and society rather than to separate them from that society. Here the group is facilitating and affirming its members' prior identities. . .

The common elements which emerge from the JPS interviews are a fundamentalist Christian background, a falling away from commitment to God and to parents, continued involvement in schools and/or jobs, and a renewal of the original commitments.

> Gordon, D. F., 'Identity and social commitment' in Mor, H. (ed.), *Identity and Religion*, Sage Publications Ltd., London, 1978.

Questions

1 Sects are usually associated with deprived sections of the population. Is there any evidence of this in the extracts?
2 What functions might sects serve for their members?
3 Given the numbers of people attracted to sects, how significant are the claims made by Glock and Bellah that these new religious movements might serve integrative functions?
4 Is there any indication in the extracts that sects might be the forerunners of political awareness and social change?

CHESTER COLLEGE LIBRARY

Further reading

Berger, P., *The Sacred Canopy*, Doubleday, New York, 1967.
Berger discusses religion in the context of a system of beliefs
which serve to provide a sense of order and consistency
amongst the apparent chaos and uncertaintly of life.

Berger, P., and Luckmann, T., Sociology of religion and
sociology of knowledge, *Sociology and Social Research*, Vol 47(4),
1963.
In this article the authors outline their central theme that the
sociology of religion has been preoccupied with the institutional context. They argue that religion is the process of
constructing 'universes of meaning' and should be studied
alongside the sociology of knowledge.

Glasner, P. E., *The Sociology of Secularisation*, Routledge and
Kegan Paul, London, 1977.
Glasner's critique of the 'secularisation myth' provides an
alternative interpretation to that of Bryan Wilson.

Glock, G. Y. and Bellah, R. N. (eds), *The New Religious
Consciousness*, University of California Press, California, 1976.
The editors have brought together a series of articles concern-
ing research carried out into religious movements in the San
Francisco Bay area in the 1970s. The book contains some
interesting articles on Krishna Consciousness, 3HO and the
Synanon Organisation, as well as separate chapters from
Glock and Bellah drawing the research together.

Harris, M., *Cows, Pigs, Wars and Witches*, Hutchinson, London,
1975.
This is a controversial book which attempts to offer insights
and explanations for various 'religious' phenomena, offering
'rational' explanations for the Hindu taboo on cow slaughter,
the Jewish taboo on pork and so on.

Hill, M., *A Sociology of Religion*, Heinemann Educational Books,
London, 1973.

This is a general text on the subject with a useful discussion of the Halevy thesis.

Luckmann, T., *Life-World and Social Realities*, Heinemann Educational Books, 1983.
Luckmann discusses the changing nature of religious beliefs in contemporary society in the context of the general views expressed jointly with Berger.

Marshall, G., *In Search of the Spirit of Capitalism*, Hutchinson, London, 1982.
This book provides perhaps the best, and one of the most up to date, commentaries on the 'Protestant Ethic' thesis.

McGuire, M. B., *Religion: the social context*, Wadsworth Publishing Co., California, 1981.
Although this covers many of the major themes in the sociology of religion, the book offers a particularly comprehensive outline of the debate concerning religion and social change, and begins to explore the factors which might affect whether religion is change inducing or change inhibiting.

Scharf, B.R., *The Sociological Study of Religion*, Hutchinson, London, 1970.
This remains one of the most comprehensive and useful introductions to the sociology of religion.

Turner, B. S., *Religion and Social Theory*, Heinemann Educational Books, London, 1983.
This is a general text which provides, amongst other things, links between the theoretical issues raised by the founding fathers and more recent research.

Weber, M., *The Protestant Ethic and the Spirit of Capitalism*, Unwin University Books, London, 1974.
Weber's account of the connection between Calvinism and the spirit of capitalism is perhaps the most accessible of the works of the classical sociologists, and remains the centre of one of the most important debates in sociology.

Wilson, B. R., *Religion in Sociological Perspective*, Oxford University Press, Oxford, 1982.
Bryan Wilson remains one of the major proponents of the secularisation thesis. This book, which is based on a series of lectures he gave in Tokyo in 1979, contains useful outlines of

his views on religious sects, the functions of religion in contemporary society, and the secularisation debate.

Worsley, P., *The Trumpet Shall Sound*, MacGibbon and Kee, London, 1957.

Worsley provides a Marxian analysis of 'cargo cults' and argues that they can be understood as a reaction to colonialism and exploitation, and may be the forerunners of political awareness.

Index